Quick & Easy Way To Learn Korean

Shyam Kumar Anand
Jawaharlal Nehru University

G T BOOK AGENCY

ISBN : 81-87838-12-4
ISBN : 978-81-87838-12-8

Reprinted 2025

Quick & Easy Way to Learn Korean

Published by
Qualis Books
140, Medha Apartment
Mayur Vihar, Ext. Phase 1,
New Delhi - 110091
E-mail : qualisbooks@yahoo.co.in

Printed in India at
DK Fine Art Press
New Delhi.

Quick & Easy Way to Learn Korean

This book is intended for any reader who wishes to learn Korean language and culture in 'Quick and Easy Way' just for one's personal interest as a student, or is about to travel to this beautiful island nation. As a result, the grammar and the vocabulary have been confined as per the relevance to such a reader with the objective of self learning and where the process does not become a 'put off' on coming across too much of grammar rules.

In order to facilitate the pronunciations, each word and sentence in Korean is followed by its possible equivalent pronunciation in English. Although, it is not possible to include all the aspects but sincere effort has been made to include the most common aspects.

In publishing this book, I am thankful to 'Qualis Books' and my Korean friend Mun Eunseong who have provided me their unconditional support and assistance.

I hope this book will be useful for everyone who has some interest and wish to learn the "Basics of Korean".

Good Luck!

Contents

Korean Alphabets

한국어알파벳 (hangu-ga alpha-bet)

Alphabets	Pronunciation	
ㄱ	khiyok	K (as in Kiss, but relaxed)
ㄲ	sang khiyok	k (as in skull, tense)
ㄴ	niyon	n (as in nose)
ㄷ	thigot	t (as in tall, but relaxed)
ㄸ	sang-thigot	t(as in steam, tense)
ㄹ	riyol	l (as in lung)
ㅁ	mi-yom	m (as in mother)
ㅂ	phiyop	p (as in park)
ㅃ	sang phiyop	p(as in speak)
ㅅ	shiot	s (as in soul)
ㅆ	sang shiot	s (as in sea)
ㅇ	ung	ng (as in King)

ㅈ	jieut	ch (as in chill, but relaxed)
ㅉ	sang jieut	tch (as in midget, tense)
ㅊ	chieut	ch (as in change, aspirated)
ㅋ	khiyok	k (as in King, aspirated)
ㅌ	tieut	t (as in talk, aspirated)
ㅍ	pieup	p (as in pill)
ㅎ	hieut	h (as in hope)

Vowels

Alphabets	Pronunciation
ㅏ	a (as in father)
ㅐ	a (as in care)
ㅑ	ya (as in yard)
ㅒ	ya (as in yankie)
ㅓ	uh (as in uh-oh)
ㅔ	e (as in met)
ㅕ	yo (as in yonder)
ㅖ	ye (as in yes)

ㅗ	**o (as in home)**
ㅘ	**wa (as in wine)**
ㅙ	**wae (as in wait)**
ㅚ	**we (as in wet)**
ㅛ	**yo (as in yoga)**
ㅜ	**oo (as in boo)**
ㅝ	**wo (as in wonder)**
ㅞ	**whe (as in when)**
ㅟ	**wi (as in we are the world)**
ㅠ	**yu (as in you)**
ㅡ	**u (as in pull)**
ㅢ	**ui (u as in pull, followed by ee as in feet, but said quickly as one sound)**
ㅣ	**ee (as in feet)**

Korean Grammar Rules : Sentence Structure

In Korean, the order of the words in a sentence is subject + object + verb.

Politeness and respect to seniority is a critical part of Korean culture and the Korean Language.

Korean Grammar Rules: Nouns and Pronouns

Korean Nouns do not have a Gender. Korean Nouns can be made plural by adding "들"

Korean Pronouns have honorifics to show respect formally or informally.

Korean Nouns rely on several factors such as tense, aspects, mood, and the social relation to the people you are referring and speaking to.

Using the wrong honorific noun can be considered insulting to the person you are speaking to. The honorific suffix – 님 (nim) is common suffix added to such respect to someone's family.

Example : Grandfather

할아버지(hal-abeoji)

Can be said to your own grandfather

할아버님(hal-abeonim)

when showing respect to your own grandfather or referring to someone else's grandfather.

Korean Grammar Rules: Verbs

Korean Verbs uses three tenses: past, present, and future Verbs can change according to the age and/or seniority to the person your speaking to.

Korean Verbs rely on several factors such as tense, aspect, mood, and the social relation to the people you are referring and speaking to.

Most Korean verbs have base form and can be made honorific by adding the infix "시 (si)" or 으시 (eusi) in the middle of the word.

Examples of Korean Verbs

English	Basic Korean	Honorific Korean
to do	하다 (hada)	하시다 (hasida)
To go	가다 (gada)	가시다 (ga-sida)
To call	부르다(bu+-reu-da)	부으시다(bu-reu-sida)

Korean Grammar Rules: Adjectives

Korean Adjectives are words that describe or modify another person or thing in the sentence

Korean Adjective Examples:

미인 (mi-in) – beautiful women

검은책 (geom-un chekh)- black book

파란접시 (paran-jeob-si)- blue plate

나쁜하루 (nap-peun haru)- bad day

CHAPTER-2

Parts of the Body

인체의일부분 (Inche ei ilbubun)

English	Korean	Pronunciation
Abdomen	복부	Bokbu
Ankle	발목	Balmok
Appendix	맹장	Maengjang
Arm	팔	Pal
Armpit	겨드랑이	Gueodeurangi
Back	등	Deung
Beard	턱수염	Teok-suyeom
Belly	배	Bae
Bladder	방광	Bang-gwang
Blood	피	Pi

Body	몸	**mom**
Bone	뼈	**Ppyeo**
Brain	머리	**Meori**
Breast	가슴	**Gaseum**
Cheek	뺨	**Ppyam**
Chest	가슴	**Baseum**
Chin	턱	**Teok**
Collarbone	쇄골	**Swaegol**
Ear	귀	**Gwi**
Elbow	팔꿈치	**Palkkumchi**
Eye	눈	**Nun**
Eyeball	눈알	**Nun-nal**
Eyebrow	눈썹	**Nun-sseop**
Eyelash	속눈썹	**Soknunsseop**
Eyelid	눈꺼풀	**NunnkKeo-pul**

Face	얼굴	**Eol-gul**
Finger	손가락	**Son-ga-rak**
Fist	주먹	**Jumeok**
Flesh	살	**Sal**
Foot	발	**Bal**
Forehead	이마	**Ema**
Gall-bladder	담낭	**Dam-nang**
Gum	잇몸	**It-mom**
Hair	머리카락	**Morikharak**
Hand	손	**Son**
Head	머리	**Meori**
Heart	심장	**Sim-jang**
Heel	뒤꿈치	**Dwi-kkumchi**
Hip	엉덩이	**Eong-dong-e**
Intestine	창자	**Chang-ja**
Joint	관절	**Gwan-jeol**

Knee	무릎	**Mureuf**
Kidney	신장	**Sin-jang**
Large intestine	대장	**Dae-jang**
Leg	다리	**Dari**
Lip	입술	**Ip-sul**
Liver	간	**Gan**
Lung	폐	**Pye**
Moustache	콧수염	**Kot-suyeom**
Mouth	입	**Ip**
Muscle	근육	**Geun-yuk**
Nail	손톱	**Son-top**
Neck	목	**Mok**
Nerve	신경	**Singyeong**
Nose	코	**Kho**
Palm	손바닥	**Sonba-dak**
Penis	음경	**Eumgyeong**

Rib	갈비	**Galpi**
Shoulder	어깨	**Eokkae**
Sinus	부비강	**Phubi-gang**
Skin	피부	**Pibu**
Skull	두개골	**Dugae-gol**
Small intestine	소장	**Sojang**
Sole	발바닥	**Bal-pa-dak**
Spine	척추	**Cheok-chu**
Stomach	배	**Bae**
Systole	심장수축	**Simjang-suchuk**
Thigh	허벅지	**Heo-beok-ji**
Throat	목구멍	**Mok-gu-meong**
Thumb	엄지손가락	**Eom-ji son-garak**
Toe	발가락	**Bal-garak**
Tongue	혀	**Hyeo**
Tooth	이	**e**

Vein	**정맥**	**Jeong-maek**
Vertebra	**등골뼈**	**Thung-khol-pyo**
Waist	**허리**	**Hori**
Wrist	**손목**	**Son-mok**

CHAPTER-3

Climate

기후 (Gi-hu)

Cold 차갑다 (cha-gap-da)
It will be (very) cold tomorrow
내일 날씨가 추울거 같습니다.
Na-el nal-siga chu-ul-geo gat-sumnida.

Hot 덥다 (Deopda)
It was (very) hot last night.
어제 밤에 너무 더웠습니다.
Eoje phame nomu deo-wot-sumnida.

The weather is very fine.
날씨가 너무 좋습니다.
Nalsiga nomu cho-sumnida.

Good/bad weather 좋은/ 나쁜 날씨 (Joe-un nalsi / na-ppeun nalsi)

The weather is going to be bad.

날씨가 나빠 질거같습니다.

Nalsiga nappa-jil-gokath-sumnida.

What will the weather be like tomorrow?

내일 날씨가 어떨까요?

Nae-il nalsiga atol-kayo?

Sunny 햇살이 (Haetsari), Sun 해 (hae)

The sun is not shining.

해가 빛나지 않습니다.

Haega bit-naji ansum-nida.

It is pleasantly warm today.

오늘은 날씨가 따뜻합니다.

O-narun-nalsiga tatat-hamnida.

Cool 시원하다 (siwon-hada)

It is cool today.

오늘은 시원합니다.

Ona-ran siwan hamnida.

From sunrise to sunset.

일출에서 일몰까지.

Il-chul-yeso il-mul kaji.

In the sunshine.

햇빛에.

Haet-bit-e

What is the temperature (today)?

오늘 기온이 어떻습니까?

Onal khi-oni atoh-sumnikka?

The temperature is five degrees below zero (today).

오늘은 기온이 영하 5도 입니다.

Ona-ran khi-oni young-ha o-do emnida.

What is the weather forecast?

일기 예보가 어떻습니까?

ilki yebo-ga atoh-sumnikka?

What are the weather conditions of Moscow?

모스크바 날씨는 어떻습니까?

Moscow-ba nalsi-nan atoh-sumnikka?

It is windy today.

오늘은 바람이 붑니다.

Ona-ran barami phum-nida.

Animals

동물 (Dong-mul)

English	Korean	Pronunciation
Animal	동물	Dong-mul
Bull	황소	Hwang-so
Bullock	황소	Hwang-so
Buffalo	물소	Mulso
Bitch	암캐	Aam-kae
Calf	송아지	Songa-ji
Cat	고양이	Go-yang-e
Chameleon	카멜레온	Kha-mel-leon
Camel	낙타	Naktha
Cow	소	So

Dangerous	위험하다	**wehom-hada**
Deer	사슴	**sa-sum**
Dog	개	**khe**
Donkey	당나귀	**dangna-khue**
Elephant	코끼리	**kho-kiri**
Endangered	위험에 처한,	**we-homei cho-han**
Fox	여우	**ya-u**
Goat	염소	**yam-so**
Hare	산토끼	**san-thoki**
Heifer	어린암소	**aurin-amso**
Horse	말	**mal**
Hound	사냥개	**sa-nyang-khe**
Jackal	자칼	**ja-kal**
Lamb	어린양	**o-rin-yang**
Leopard	표범	**phyo-fom**
Lion	사자	**saja**

Mare	바다	**fada**
Mongoose	몽구스	**mongus**
Monkey	원숭이	**wan-sung-e**
Mouse	쥐	**chue**
Mule	노새	**no-se**
Pig	돼지	**thoye-ji**
Pup	새끼	**saegi**
Python	비단뱀	**phidan-fem**
Ram	숫양	**sut-yang**
Rhinoceros	코뿔소	**kho-ppul-so**
Sheep	양	**yang**
Skunk	스컹크	**seu-keong-keu**
Snake	뱀	**baem**
Squirrel	다람쥐	**daram-jwi**
Stag	수사슴	**sut-sa-suem**
Swine	새끼	**sae-khi**

Tiger	호랑이	**horangi**
Tom	수컷	**sukhot**
Wolf	늑대	**nuk-the**
Crab	게	**ge**
Crocodile	악어	**ak-eo**
Fish	생선	**seng-son**
Leech	거머리	**kho-mori**
Tortoise	거북	**geo-buk**

CHAPTER-5

Birds

새 (Sae)

English	Korean	Pronunciation
Bat	박쥐	bak-jwi
Bird	새	sae
Cock	수탉	su-tak
Crane	두루미, 학	du-rumi, hak
Crow	까마귀	kka-ma-gwi
Cuckoo	뻐꾸기	pho-ku-gi
Dove	비둘기	phi-tulgi
Duck	오리	o-ri
Hen	암닭	aam- tak
Owl	올빼미	ol-pae-mi

Parrot	앵무새	**yeng-mu-se**
Partridge	자고새	**jago-se**
Peacock	공작	**khong-jak**
Pigeon	비둘기	**phi-thul-gi**
Sparrow	참새	**cham-sae**
Swan	백조	**phaik-jo**
Vulture	독수리	**dak-suri**

CHAPTER-6

Insects and Crawlers

곤충과 기어 다니는것 (Khon-chung-gwa khi-o-thani-nan got)

English	Korean	Pronunciation
Ant	개미	khemi
Bee	꿀벌	khul-phol
Bug	곤충	khon-chung
Butterfly	나비	nabi
Firefly	반딧불이	phan-dit-furi
Fly	날다	nal-da
Frog	개구리	gae-ku-ri
Germ	세균	se-gyun
Insect	곤충	gon-chung

Lizard	도마뱀	**doma-baem**
Locust	메뚜기	**me-thugi**
Mosquito	모기	**mogi**
Scorpion	전갈	**chon-khal**
Spider	거미	**geomi**
Snail	달팽이	**thal-feng-e**
Wasp	말벌	**mal-beol**

Plants and Flowers

동식물 (thong-sik-mul)

English	Korean	Pronunciation
Acacia	아카시아	akhasia
Camomile	카모마일	kha-mo mile
Chrysanthemum	국화	kuk-hwa
Daisy	데이지	dezi
Jasmine	재스민	Jasmine
Lilac	라일락	ra-il-rak
Lily	백합	baek-ham
Lotus	연꽃	yon-koth
Magnolia	목련	mok-ryon
Marigold	금잔화	khum-chan-hwa

Mushroom	버섯	**pho-sat**
Narcissus	수선화	**su-son-hwa**
Rose	장미	**jang-mi**

CHAPTER-8

House and House-Hold Articles

집과 가정 용품(Jib-gwa Gajeong Yong-pum)

English	Korean	Pronunciation
Ante-chamber	대기실	thegi-sil
Apartment house	아파트	a-phat
Arch	아치	a-chi
Armchair	안락의자	anrak-eija
Attic	다락	darak
Air freshener	방향제	phang-hyang-che
Ashtray	재떨이	che-tori
Balcony	발코니	Balcony
Basket	바구니	pha-guni
Bathmat	욕실용매트	yok-sil yong met

Bathroom	욕실	**yoksil**
Bath-salts	목욕소금	**mok-yok sogum**
Bath-sheet	목욕시트	**mok-yok si-t**
Bath-towel	목욕타올	**mok-yok ta-ol**
Bathtub	목욕통	**mok-yok-tong**
Bed	침대	**chim-dae**
Bedroom	침실	**chim-sil**
Bedsheet	침대시트	**chim-de seet**
Bedspread	침대보	**chim-de-bo**
Bench	벤치	**benchi**
Blanket	담요	**dam-yo**
Bolster	긴베게	**khin-pe-ge**
Bottle	병	**phyong**
Bottle opener	병따개	**phyong-ta-khe**
Bowl	사발	**sa-bal**
Box	상자	**sang-ja**

Bracket	받침대	**pha-chim-de**
Brick	벽돌	**phyok-dol**
Broom	긴자루	**khin-ja-ru**
Brush	브러시	**brush**
Bucket	바구니	**pha-guni**
Building	건물	**khon-mul**
Bungalow	방갈로	**bungalow**
Cabinet	장식장	**khebi-net**
Candle	양초	**yang-cho**
Candlestick	촛대	**chotte**
Canister	통	**thong**
Carpet	양탄자	**yang-than-ja**
Can opener	깡통따개	**khang-thong-ta-ge**
Carpet tile	카펫타일	**kha-pet-tha-el**
Ceiling	천장	**chon-jang**

Censer	**향로**	**hyang-ro**
Chair	**의자**	**uija**
Chandelier	**샹들리에**	**syangdul-ri-a**
Chimney	**굴뚝**	**khul-tuk**
Chopping-board	**도마**	**thoma**
Cigarette	**담배**	**thambe**
Lighter	**라이터**	**khorut-pe**
Closet	**벽장**	**byeok-jang**
Clothes-basket	**세탁물바구니**	**se-thak-mul ba-guni**
Clothes-brush	**옷솔**	**ot-sol**
Clothes-drier	**빨래건조기**	**palle-khon-chogi**
Clothes-hanger	**옷걸이**	**ot-khori**
Clothes-line	**빨랫줄**	**pallet-chul**
Clothes peg	**기성복**	**khi-song,phok**
Clothes rack	**옷걸이**	**ot-khori**

Compact disk	컴팩트디스크	**khompact-deesk**
Computer	컴퓨터	**kham-phu-ta**
Corridor	복도	**phok-do**
Cottage	작은집	**cha-gun chib**
Couch	소파	**so-pa**
Courtyard	안마당	**an-madang**
Cup	컵	**keop**
Cupboard	찬장	**chan-jang**
Curtain	커튼	**keo-teun**
Cushion	쿠션	**khu-syon**
Door	문	**mun**
Doorbell	초인종	**cho-in-jong**
Door chain	도어체인	**do-o chaen**
Doorframe	문틀	**mun-teul**
Doorstep	문간	**mun-gan**
Drain	배수를하다	**phe-su-rul hada**

Drawer	서랍	**so-rap**
Drawing room	거실	**kho-sil**
Dressing table	화장대	**hwa-jang-the**
Eaves	처마	**cho-ma**
Fan	선풍기	**sun-phungi**
Finger bowl	핑거볼	**fingo-ful**
Floor	바닥	**pha-dak**
Fork	포크	**phok**
Foundation	기초, 토대	**khi-jo, tho-de**
Frying pan	프라이팬	**fry-phain**
Funnel	깔때기	**khal-te-gi**
Gallery	갤러리	**khello-ri**
Gas-cooker	가스레인지	**khas-reinji**
Gas-cylinder	가스용기	**khas-yongi**
Glass	유리	**yuri**
Hall	복도	**phok-do**

Hand wash	손세척	**son-se-chok**
Hearth	난로	**nan-lo**
House	집	**chib**
Inkpot	잉크병	**ing-keu-beong**
Jar	단지	**dan-ji**
Jug	주전자	**ju-jeon-ja**
Key	열쇠	**yal-se**
Kitchen	부엌	**phu-yak**
Knife	칼	**khal**
Knife (folding)	접히는칼	**chop-hi-nan khal**
Ladle	국자	**kuk-ja**
Lamp	등	**thong**
Lid	뚜껑	**thu-kong**
Lock	자물쇠	**cha-mul-se**
Match	경기	**khyongi**
Mattress	매트리스	**methriss**

Medicine cabinet	약장	**yak-jang**
Microwave oven	전자레인지	**choncha-reinji**
Mug	잔	**jan**
Mug (beer)	맥주잔	**mekju-jan**
Needle	바늘	**pha-nul**
Oven	오븐	**o-bun**
Peel	나무주걱	**namu-chugok**
Peephole	작은구멍	**cha-gun khu-mong**
Plate	접시	**chop-si**
Quilt	누비이불	**numbi-ebul**
Radio	라디오	**ra-dio**
Railing	난간	**nan-gan**
Refrigerator	냉장고	**neng-jango**
Rocking-chair	흔들 의자	**hundul-ueja**
Roof	지붕	**jibung**
Room	방	**bang**

Rope	줄	**jul**
Sack	부대	**bu-dae**
Safe	안전한	**aan-chon-han**
Saucepan	냄비	**nembi**
Shed	흘리다	**hullida**
Shower	샤워	**sha-wa**
Sieve	소쿠리	**so-khu-ri**
Sink (kitchen)	싱크대	**sinkh-de**
Sofa-bed	소파–침대	**so-fa chim-de**
Spoon	숟가락	**sut-kha-rak**
Stair	계단	**khe-dan**
Stick	막대기	**mak-the-gi**
Stone	돌	**dol**
Stool	발판	**phal-faan**
Storey	층	**chung**
Stove	난로	**nan-lo**

String	**끈**	**khun**
Studio apartment	**원룸**	**one-rum**
Table	**식탁**	**sik-thak**
Table cloth	**식탁보**	**sik-thak-bo**
Tea cloth	**행주**	**heng-ju**
Teacup	**차잔**	**cha−chan**
Teakettle	**차주전자**	**cha-chuchon-ja**
Television	**텔레비전**	**thele-bhijon**
Thimble	**골무**	**khol-mu**
Tile	**타일**	**tha-el**
Tissue paper	**박엽지**	**pha-gyob-ji**
Toaster	**토스터**	**tho[illegible]ta**
Tongs	**집게**	**chib-g[illegible]**
Torch	**손전등**	**son−jon−dung**
Tray	**쟁반**	**jeng-phan**
Tumbler	**텀블러**	**Tumbler**

Umbrella	우산	**usan**
Urinal	소변기	**so-phyon-gi**
Vase	꽃병	**kot-byong**
Wall	벽	**phyok**
Wall-painting	벽화	**phyok-hwa**
Washing-machine	세탁기	**se-thak-gi**
Washing-powder	세제	**se-je**
Wick	심지	**simji**
Window	창문	**chang-mun**

Toiletries

세면용품 (se-myeon yong-pum)

English	Korean	Pronunciation
Brush	솔	sol
Dandruff	비듬	phi-dum
Shampoo	샴푸	Shampoo
Deodorant	데오도런트	Deodorant
Mouth-wash	구강 청결제	khu-khang chong-gyol-che
Perfume	향수	hyang-su
Razor	면도기	myon-do-gi
Razor (electric)	전기면도기	jeon-gi myon-do-gi
Roll-on	롤온	rol-on

Scissors	가위	**kha-ue**
Shaving brush	면도 솔	**myon-do-sol**
Shaving cream	면도 크림	**myon-do-khurim**
Soap	비누	**phi-nu**
Sunblock	썬 블록	**Sunblock**
Suntan lotion	선탠 로션	**son-than lo-sun**
Tooth brush	칫솔	**chit-sol**
Tooth paste	치약	**chi-yak**
Tooth powder	가루치약	**kharu-chi-yak**
Towel	수건	**su-gon**
Underpants	속바지	**sok-phaji**
Undergarments	속옷	**sok-oat**

School

학교 (hak-yo)

I am studying business.
저는 비즈니스를 공부하고 있어요.
Chonan biz-nis-rul khombu-hago eso-yo.

I am studying at the college.
저는 대학에서 공부하고 있어요.
Chonan dehak-yeso khombu-hago eso-yo.

What grade are you in?
당신은 몇 학년 이예요?
Thang-si-nan myot hang-nyon e-ae-yo?

What do you do after school?
당신은 학교 끝나고 무엇을해요?
Thang-si-nan hakyo kun-nago mu-asul haiyo?

Is there a creche here?
여기에 탁아소가 있어요?
Yagi-ye thaga-soga eso-yo?

Where is the playground?
운동장은 어디에 있어요?
Un-dong-jang-un audiye eso-yo?

Are there swings in the school?
학교에 그네가 있어요?
Hakyo-ye kun-nega eso-yo?

Clothing

의류 (ye-ryu)

English	Korean	Pronunciation
Apron	앞치마	af-chima
Bathing-cap	목욕모자	mok-yog moja
Bathing-suit	수영복	su-yong-bok
Bathrobe	목욕가운	mo-gyok kha-un
Belt	벨트	Belt
Bikini	비키니	Bikini
Blanket	담요	tham-yo
Blouse	블라우스	bal-la-us
Blue jeans	청바지	chong-phaji
Bodice	조끼	cho-ki
Boots	부츠	Boots

Border	테두리	**the−thu−ri**
Bra	브라	**Bra**
Brocade	양단	**yang−dan**
Button	단추	**than-ju**
Canvas	화폭	**hwa−phok**
Cap	모자	**moja**
Cardigan	카디건	**kha−di−gon**
Cashmere	캐시미어	**khesi−mio**
Cloak	망토	**mang−tho**
Cloth	옷	**oat**
Coat	외투	**we−thu**
Corduroy	코듀로이	**kho−du−roe**
Corset	코르셋	**khor−set**
Damask	리넨	**li−nen**
Darning	짜깁기	**chha−gip−gi**

Dress	**드레스**	**Dress**
Flannel	**플란넬**	**Flannel**
Gloves	**장갑**	**chang-gaap**
Handkerchief	**손수건**	**son-su-gon**
Hat	**모자**	**moja**
Jacket	**재킷**	**Jacket**
Jersey	**저지**	**cho-ji**
Lace	**레이스**	**Lace**
Leather jacket	**가죽재킷**	**kha-juk-jekit**
Lingerie	**속옷**	**sok-oat**
Lining	**안감**	**aan-gam**
Muffler	**목도리**	**mok-thori**
Napkin	**냅킨**	**Napkin**
Nightgown	**잠옷**	**jam-ot**
Pajamas	**파자마**	**pha-jama**

Pants	**바지**	**baji**
Panties	**팬티**	**Panties**
Petticoat	**속치마**	**sok-chima**
Pocket	**주머니**	**chu-moni**
Polyester	**폴리 에스테르**	**folli-ester**
Raincoat	**우비**	**u-bi**
Sackcloth	**삼베옷**	**sam-be-ot**
Scarf	**스카프**	**as-kaf**
Shawl	**숄**	**syol**
Shirt	**셔츠**	**Shirt**
Skirt	**치마**	**chima**
Sleeve	**소매**	**so-me**
Sportswear	**운동복**	**un-dong-bok**
Stitching	**바느질**	**phan-chil**
Stocking	**스타킹**	**as-tha-king**
Suit	**한벌**	**han-bol**

Tie	넥타이	**nek-tha-e**
Tie clip	넥타이핀	**nek-tha-e-pin**
Tunic	튜닉	**thyu-nik**
Towel	수건	**su-gon**
Trousers	바지	**ba-ji**
Turban	터번	**tho-bun**
Underpants	속바지	**sok-baji**
Veil	면사포	**myon-sa-pho**
Yarn	실	**sil**

Numbers

숫자 (Sutza)

	English	Korean	Pronunciation
1	one	일	il
2	two	이	e
3	three	삼	sam
4	four	사	sa
5	five	오	O
6	six	육	yuk
7	seven	칠	chil
8	eight	팔	pal
9	nine	구	gu
10	ten	십	sip

11	eleven	십일	sip-il
12	twelve	십이	sip-e
13	thirteen	십삼	sip-sam
14	fourteen	십사	sip-sa
15	fifteen	십오	sip-o
16	sixteen	십육	sip-yuk
17	seventeen	십칠	sip-chil
18	eighteen	십팔	sip-pal
19	nineteen	십구	sip-gu
20	twenty	이십	e-sip
21	twenty one	이십일	e-sip-il
22	twenty two	이십이	e-sip-e
23	twenty three	이십삼	e-sip-sam
24	twenty four	이십사	e-sip-sa
25	twenty five	이십오	e-sip-o
26	twenty six	이십육	e-sip-yuk

27	twenty seven	이십칠	e-sip-chil
28	twenty eight	이십육	e-sip-pal
29	twenty nine	이십구	e-sip-gu
30	thirty	삼십	sam-sip
31	thirty one	삼십일	sam-sip-il
32	thirty two	삼십이	sam-sip-e
33	thirty three	삼십삼	sam-sip-sam
34	thirty four	삼십사	sam-sip-sa
35	thirty five	삼십오	sam-sip-o
36	thirty six	삼십육	sam-sip-yuk
37	thirty seven	삼십칠	sam-sip-chil
38	thirty eight	삼십팔	sam-sip-phal
39	thirty nine	삼십구	sam-sip-khu
40	forty	사십	sa-sip
41	forty one	사십일	sa-sip-il
42	forty two	사십이	sa-sip-e

43	**forty three**	**사십삼**	**sa-sip-sam**
44	**forty four**	**사십사**	**sa-sip-sa**
45	**forty five**	**사십오**	**sa-sip-o**
46	**forty six**	**사십육**	**sa-sip-yuk**
47	**forty seven**	**사십칠**	**sa-sip-chil**
48	**forty eight**	**사십팔**	**sa-sip-phal**
49	**forty nine**	**사십구**	**sa-sip-khu**
50	**fifty**	**오십**	**o-sip**
51	**fifty one**	**오십일**	**o-sip-il**
52	**fifty two**	**오십이**	**o-sip-e**
53	**fifty three**	**오십삼**	**o-sip-sam**
54	**fifty four**	**오십사**	**o-sip-sa**
55	**fifty five**	**오십오**	**o-sip-o**
56	**fifty six**	**오십육**	**o-sip-yuk**
57	**fifty seven**	**오십칠**	**o-sip-chil**
58	**fifty eight**	**오십팔**	**o-sip-phal**

59	fifty nine	오십구	o-sip-khu
60	sixty	육십	yuk-sip
61	sixty one	육십일	yuk-sip-il
62	sixty two	육십이	yuk-sip-e
63	sixty three	육십삼	yuk-sip-sam
64	sixty four	육십사	yuk-sip-sa
65	sixty five	육십오	yuk-sip-o
66	sixty six	육십육	yuk-sip-yuk
67	sixty seven	육십칠	yuk-sip-chil
68	sixty eight	육십팔	yuk-sip-phal
69	sixty nine	육십구	yuk-sip-khu
70	seventy	칠십	chil-sip
71	seventy one	칠십일	chil-sip-il
72	seventy two	칠십이	chil-sip-e
73	seventy three	칠십삼	chil-sip-sam
74	seventy four	칠십사	chil-sip-sa
75	seventy five	칠십오	chil-sip-o

76	seventy six	칠십육	chil-sip-yuk
77	seventy seven	칠십칠	chil-sip-chil
78	seventy eight	칠십팔	chil-sip-phal
79	seventy nine	칠십구	chil-sip-khu
80	eighty	팔십	phal-sip
81	eighty one	팔십일	phal-sip-il
82	eighty two	팔십이	phal-sip-e
83	eighty three	팔십삼	phal-sip-sam
84	eighty four	팔십사	phal-sip-sa
85	eighty five	팔십오	phal-sip-o
86	eighty six	팔십육	phal-sip-yuk
87	eighty seven	팔십칠	phal-sip-chil
88	eighty eight	팔십팔	phal-sip-phal
89	eighty nine	팔십구	phal-sip-khu
90	ninety	구십	khu-sip
91	ninety one	구십일	khu-sip-il
92	ninety two	구십이	khu-sip-e

93	ninety three	구십삼	khu-sip-sam
94	ninety four	구십사	khu-sip-sa
95	ninety five	구십오	khu-sip-o
96	ninety six	구십육	khu-sip-yuk
97	ninety seven	구십칠	khu-sip-chil
98	ninety eight	구십팔	khu-sip-phal
99	ninety nine	구십구	khu-sip-khu
100	hundred	백	baek
101	one hundred one	백일	baek-il
200	two hundred	이백	e-baek
1000	one thousand	천	cheon
1002	one thousand two	천이	cheon-e
2000	two thousand	이천	e-chon
10000	ten thousand	만	man
100000	one lakh	십만	sip-man
1000000	ten lakhs	백만	baek-man

CHAPTER-13

Money & Currency Exchange

돈및환전 (thon-mith-hwan-jon)

English	Russian	Pronunciation
Currency	통화	thong-hwa
Currency market	통화시장	thong-hwa-sijang
Currency note	통화참고	thong-hwa-cham-go
Currency restrictions	통화제한	thong-hwa che-han
Currency unit	통화단위	thong-hwa than-ue
One dollar bill	1 달러계산서	1-dallo-khesan-so
Dollar rate	달러환율	dallo-hwan-yul
Dollar sign	달러기호	dallo-khi-ho
Foreign exchange	외국환	wei-guk-hwan
Exchange rate	환율	hwan-yul
Traveller's cheque	여행자수표	yo-heng-ja su-phyo

Where can I change some money?
어디에서 환전 할수 있습니까?
Audi-yeso hwan-jon hal-su yi-sum-nikka?

What is the exchange rate?
환율은 어떻게 됩니까?
Hwan-yu-ran ata-khe thoyem-nikka?

I am out of cash./ I haven't any cash.
저는 현금이 없습니까.
Cho-nan hyon-gum-e op-sumnikka.

What's the charge for that?
그비용은 얼마 입니까?
Khu phi-yong-un olma-imnikka?

You may keep the change.
잔돈으로 바꿔 주실 수 있으세요?.
Chang-thon-uro fak-kua chu-sil su yi-sa-seyo?

I would like to change money.
잔돈으로 바꿔 주세요.
Chan-thon-ro fa-kua chu-sayo.

I would like to change a traveller's cheque.
여행자 수표를 변경하고 싶습니다.
Na-nan yo-heng-ja su-phyo-rul phyon.

I would like to change 5000 rupees into won.
5000 루피를 환전하고 싶어요.
o-chon rupi hwan-chon hago si-phayo.

Where is the nearest ATM?
가장 가까운 ATM이 어디에 있어요?.
Kha-jang kakka-un ATM-e audi-a eso-yo?

Can I use my credit card to withdraw money?
신용카드로 돈을 인출 할수 있어요?
Sin-yong khad-ro thon-ul in-chul hal-su eso-yo?

CHAPTER-14

Time

시간 (si-gan)

English	Korean	Pronunciation
Afternoon	오후에	o-hu-ye
An hour	한 시간	han−sigan
Anniversary	기념일	khi−nyom−il
At times	가끔	ka−kum
Century	세기	segi
Dawn	새벽	se−phyok
Day	낮	nat
Day to day	나날의	na−nare
Decade	십년	sip−nyon
Evening	저녁	cha−nyok

Fortnight	이주일	**e-chu-il**
Hour	시간	**si-gan**
Late	늦다	**nut-ta**
Leap year	윤년	**yun-nyon**
Midday	한낮	**han-nat**
Midnight	한밤중	**han-pham-chung**
Minute	분	**bun**
Morning	아침	**a-chim**
New year	새해	**se-he**
New year's eve	섣달 그믐	**sot-tal khu-mum**
Period	기간	**khi-gan**
Second	초	**cho**
Sometimes	때때로	**te-te-ro**
Time	시간	**si-gan**

Present 현재 (hyeon-jae)

Now	지금	chi-gum
Nowadays	요즘	yo-jum
Right now	바로 지금	pharo-chigum
This afternoon	오늘 오후	o-nal o-hu
This month	이번 달	e-bon-tal
This morning	오늘 아침	onal-a-chim
This week	이번 주	e-bon-chu
This year	올해	ol-hei
Today	오늘	o-nal
Tonight	오늘 밤	o-nal-pham
Past	과거	(khwa-go)
Day before yesterday	그저께	khu-chho-ke
Last night	어제 밤	aje-pham
Last time	지난 시간	chi-nan si-gan

Last week	지난 주	**chi-nan chhu**
Last year	작년	**chang-nyon**
Since	부터	**bu-tho**
The year before	작년에	**chang-nyo-ne**
Two days ago	이틀전	**e-thul-jun**
Yesterday	어제	**a-jey**
Yesterday afternoon	어제 오후	**a-jey o-hu**
Yesterday evening	어제 저녁	**a-jey cho-nyok**
Yesterday morning	어제 아침	**a-jey a-chim**

Future미래 (mire)

Day after tomorrow	모레	**more**
In a month	달에	**ta-re**
In an hour	한 시간 후	**han-sigan-hu**
In five minutes	오분의	**o-bun-e**
In two days	이틀 후에	**e-dul hu-ye**

Next month	다음 달	**tha-um tal**
Next week	다음 주	**tha-um chu**
Next year	내년에	**ne-nyon-ne**
Tomorrow	내일	**ne-il**
Tomorrow afternoon	내일 오후	**ne-il-o-hu**
Tomorrow evening	내일 저녁	**ne-il cho-nyok**
Tomorrow morning	내일 아침	**ne-il-a-chim**
Until	~까지	**kaji**

What is the time?
몇 시 입니까?
Myot-si emnikka?

Its 1 o'clock.
1시 입니다,
Han-si emnida.

Its 2 o'clock.

2시 입니다.

Thu-si emnida.

Its half past 9.

9시 반 입니다.

a-hop si phan emnida.

Its quarter past 8.

8시 15분입니다.

Yadal si sip-o bun emnida.

Its quarter to six.

5시 45 분 입니다.

Tha-sat sisam-sip-o bun 입니다.

Its 10 to 7.

6시 50 분 입니다.

Yasat si o-sip bun emnida.

At 10 a.m.

오전 열 시 입니다.

o-jan yal si emnida.

At 3 p.m sharp.

오후 세 시 입니다.

o-hu se si emnida.

The train/bus leaves at 16:45.

기차 / 버스는 4시 45분에 출발합니다.

Khicha/bus-nan ne-si sa-sip-o bune chul-bal hamnida.

Until 10 (ten) o'clock.

열 시 까지

Yal si kaji

Its late.

늦었습니다.

Nu-jat-sumnida.

※ CHAPTER-15 ※

Week

일주일 (il-chu-il)

English	Korean	Pronunciation
Monday	월요일	waryo-il
Tuesday	화요일	wayo-il
Wednesday	수요일	suyo-il
Thursday	목요일	mogyo-il
Friday	금요일	khumyo-il
Saturday	토요일	thoyo-il
Sunday	일요일	iryo-il

Tomorrow is Friday.
내일은 금요일입니다.
Ne-ir-ran khumyo-il imnida.

On Monday.

월요일에.

Waryo-ire

On Tuesday.

화요일에

Wayo-ire

Months

월 (w–al)

English	Korean	Pronunciation
January	1월	ir–wal
February	2월	e–wal
March	3월	sam–wal
April	4월	sa–wal
May	5월	o–wal
June	6월	yuk–wal
July	7월	chirl–wal
August	8월	phar–wal
September	9월	khu–wal
October	10월	sip–wal
November	11월	sip–ir–wal
December	12월	sip–e–wal

Date

날짜 (nal–cha)

What is the date today?
오늘은 며칠 입니까?
Ona–ran myot–chil imnikka?

Today's the 23rd march.
오늘은 3월 23일입니다.
Ona–ran sam–wal e–sip–sam–il imnida.

On the 3rd of this month/of next month.
이 달의 3일/ 다음 달의 3일.
e–tare sam–il/tha–um tare sam–il.

Until 6th may.
5월 6일까지.
o–wal yuk–il kaji.

CHAPTER-18

Hobbies

취미 (chu-e-mi)

English	Korean	Pronunciation
Cooking	요리하다	yori-hada
Dancing	무용	mu-yong
Gardening	정원관리	chong-won gwan-li
Hiking	하이킹	hi-khing
Pub crawls	술집 순례	sul-chib sun-le
Reading	읽기	il-ki
Shopping	쇼핑	shopping
Socializing	사교	sa-gyo
Sport	스포츠	sport
Travelling	여행	yo-heng

Do you like travelling?

당신은 여행을 좋아합니까?

Thang-si-nan yo-heng-ul choha-hamnikka?

Do you like playing an instrument?

당신은 악기 연주하는 것을 좋아합니까?

Thang-si-nan akki yon-ju ha-nan-go-sul choha-hamnikka?

Do you like singing?

당신은 노래 부르는 것을 좋아합니까?

Thang-si-nan nore-furnan gosul choha-hamnikka?

Do you like listening to music?

당신은 음악을 듣는 것을 좋아합니까?

Thang-si-nan umak-ul thu-nan gosul choha-hamnikka?

Do you like watching movies?
당신은 영화 보는 것을 좋아합니까?
Thang-si-nan yong-wa fonun gosul fogo choha-hamnikka?

Do you like going concerts?
당신은 콘서트에 가는 것을 좋아합니까?
Thang-si-nan kon-serte-khanan gosul choha-hamnikka?

What music do you like?
당신은 어떤 음악을 좋아합니까?
Thang-si-nan ottan umak-ul choha-hamnikka?

CHAPTER-19

Relationships

관계 (gwan-ge)

English	Korean	Pronunciation
Relationships	관계	khowan gae
Adopted	입양되다	yibyang tweda
Aunt	고모/이모	khomo/yimo
Boyfriend	남자친구	namza chingu
Bride	신부	sinbu
Bridegroom	신랑	sinlang
Brother	형/오빠	hyong/oppa
Brother-in-law	처남	chonam
Cousin	사촌	sachon
Daughter	딸	tal

Daughter-in-law	며느리	**myonari**
Elder brother	형	**hyong**
Elder sister	언니	**on ni**
Family	가족	**khazog**
Father	아버지	**aabozi**
Father-in-law	시아버지	**si aabozi**
Fiancé	약혼자	**yakh honza**
Fiancée	약혼녀	**yakh hon nyo**
Girlfriend	여자친구	**yoza chingu**
Grandchildren	손주	**sonzu**
Granddaughter	손녀	**son nyo**
Grandparents	조부모	**cho pumo**
Grandson	손자	**sonza**
Guest	손님	**son nim**

Host	주인	**juin**
Husband	남편	**namfyon**
Mother	어머니	**omoni**
Mother-in-law	장모	**Jangmo**
Neighbor	이웃	**eout**
Nephew	조카	**chokha**
Niece	조카딸	**chokha tal**
Parents	부모	**phumo**
Relative	친척	**chinchok**
Sister	자매	**jame**
Son	아들	**aadul**
Son-in-law	사위	**sawi**
Spouse	배우자	**baeuja**
Twin brother/sister	쌍둥이	**sang-thung-e**
Uncle	삼촌	**samchon**
Wedding	결혼	**khyolhon**

Widow	과부	**khowa bu**
Widower	홀아비	**horabhi**
Wife	아내	**aane**
Younger brother	남동생	**nam dong sheng**
Younger sister	여동생	**yodong sheng**

CHAPTER-20

Sports

스포츠 (Sports)

English	Korean	Pronunciation
Abseiling	현수하강하다	hyonsu hagang hada
Ace	에이스	ace
Athlete	선수	sonsu
Badminton	배드민턴	badminton
Ball	공	khong
Basketball	농구	nongu
Bat	배트	bat
Bungee	번지	ponzi
Jumping	점프	zomfu
Bullfight	투우	thuwoo

Card game	카드게임	**cardu game**
Caving	동굴탐험	**thongul thamhom**
Champion	챔피언	**champion**
Championship	챔피언전	**cham fiyon zon**
Coach	코치	**coachi**
Corner	모서리	**mosori**
Cricket	크리켓	**cricket**
Cricketer	크리켓선수	**cruikhet sonsu**
Cycling	자전거타기	**chazon go thagi**
Defeat	패배하다	**febehada**
Free kick	프리킥	**free kick**
Football	축구	**chukhu**
Foul	파울	**pha-ul**
Game	게임	**game**
Game fishing	낚시	**nak-si**
Goal	골문	**golmun**

Goalkeeper	골키퍼	**goalkeeper**
Golf	골프	**golf**
Group	그룹	**group**
Hockey	하키	**haki**
Judo	유도	**yudo**
Taekwondo	태권도	**taekwondo**
Ludo	루도	**ludo**
Match	경기	**khyongi**
Mountain biking	산악사이클링	**sanakh sy khuling**
Offside	오프사이드	**offside**
Penalty	처벌	**chobol**
Pass	지나가다	**china khada**
Player	선수	**sonsu**
Playground	운동장	**undong zang**
Racket	라켓	**racket**

Rock climbing	**암벽등반**	**aam byokh thungban**
Serve	**서버**	**sobo**
Snakes-ladders	**뱀사다리**	**fam sadari**
Sportsman	**선수**	**sonsu**
Surfing	**서핑**	**surfing**
Swimmer	**수영선수**	**suyong-son-su**
Swimming	**수영**	**suyong**
Team	**팀**	**team**
Tennis	**테니스**	**tennis**
Tennis-court	**테니스코트**	**tenisu khort**
Victory	**승리**	**sungni**
Volleyball	**배구**	**baegu**
Water-skis	**수상스키**	**susang sukhi**
Winner	**우승자**	**osungza**
Wrestling	**레슬링**	**resuling**

Do you like sport?
당신은 스포츠를 좋아합니까?
Thangshinun sufochu rul chohaheyo?

Yes, very much.
네, 너무 좋아해요.
Ye, nomu chohaheyo.

Not really.
아니요, 안 좋아해요.
Aniyo. Aan chohaheyo.

Would you like to go to a cricket match?
당신은 크리켓 경기에가 보고 싶어요?
Thang-shi-nun criket khyongi-ye kha fogo sifoyo?

What is the score now?
지금 점수가 어떻게돼요?
Chigum chom-su-ga otto-khe do-yo?

It's a draw/love.
이건 그림/사랑이에요.
Yigon khurim/sarang yiyeyo.

It's a match point.
이건 매치 포인트 이에요.
Yigon matchi fointh- yiyeyo.

How much time is left?
시간이 얼마나 남았어요?
Sigani olmana nama-sayo?

What sport do you play?
당신은 어떤 스포츠를 좋아해요?
Thangshin un otton sofothu rul chohaheyo?

I play...
저는 ....를좋아해요.
Chonun momo rul chohaheyo.

I follow…

저는 .....를따라해요.

Chonun momo rul chohaheyo.

I like watching sport.

저는 스포츠 보는 것을 좋아해요.

Chonun sofochu ponun khosul chohaheyo.

Which team is at the top of the league?

어느 팀이 상위에 있어요?

Anu-timi sang-we-ye yi-sayo?

Which team are you supporting?

당신이 무슨 팀을 지지해요?

Thangshinun musun thimi chiziheyo?

That was a great match!.

그건 엄청 난경기예요.!

Khugon omchongnan khyongi yeyo.

Do you want to play?
당신도 하고 싶어요?
Thang-shin-do hago sifoyo?

Can I join in?
저도 참여 할수 있을까요?
Cha-do chamyo hal su yi-sul-ka-yo?

Can I hire a racquet?
라켓을 빌릴수 있을까요?
Raket-ul fil-lil su yi-sul-kayo?

What's the charge per day?
하루에 요금이 얼마예요?
Haru-ye yogumi olma yeyo?

What's the charge per hour?
한 시간에 요금이 얼마예요?
Han sigane yogumi olma yeyo?

I would like tos cuba diving.

저는 스쿠버 다이빙을 하고싶어요

Chonun sukhubo di-bing-ul hago sifoyo?

I would like to learn to dive.

저는 다이빙을 배우고 싶어요.

Chonun dibingul pheugo sifoyo.

Where are some good diving sites?

좋은 다이빙 장소가 어디 있어요?

Choh-un dibing chang-so-ga audi yi-sayo?

Are you sure this is safe?

이건 진짜 안전 합니까?

Yigon chincha aanzon hamnikka?

Ailments

질병 (chil-byong)

English	Korean	Pronunciation
Accident	사고	**sago**
Acidity	산성	**san-song**
Acne	여드름	**yodurum**
Aids	에이즈	**aizi**
Aids test	에이즈검사	**aizi khomsa**
ailments	질병	**chilbyong**
allergy	알레르기	**aalelugi**
ambulance	구급차	**gugubcha**
anesthetic	마취제	**machwize**
antibiotics	항생제	**hangsheng ze**

antihistamines	**항히스타민제**	**hang hi sutha minze**
inflammatory	**염증**	**yom-chung**
appendicitis	**맹장염**	**mangzang yom**
asthma	**천식**	**chonsik**
baldness	**대머리**	**themori**
bandage	**붕대**	**pungde**
belching	**트림**	**thurim**
bleeding	**출혈**	**chulhyol**
blindness	**맹목**	**mengmok**
blister	**물집**	**mulzib**
blood	**피**	**fi**
blood flow	**혈류**	**hyol ryu**
blood group	**혈액형**	**hyol aekh hyong**
blood-poisoning	**패혈증**	**fehyol zung**
blood pressure	**혈압**	**hyol aab**
breath	**입김**	**ibgim**

bronchitis	**기관지염**	**khigwan chiyom**
bruise	**멍**	**mong**
burn	**불타다**	**phul thada**
cardiac	**심장**	**simzang**
arrest	**체포하다**	**chefohada**
casualty	**응급**	**ung gup**
department	**처치실**	**cho chil sil**
cataract	**폭포**	**fokfo**
chemotherapy	**항암화학요법**	**hang-aam-hwa-hak-yo-fop**
chickenpox	**소두**	**sodu**
chilblain	**동상**	**thongsang**
chill	**냉기**	**nangi**
cholera	**콜레라**	**cholera**
clinic	**진료**	**chil lyo**
colic	**신통**	**sin thong**

concussion	뇌진탕	**nwi zin thang**
condom	콘돔	**condom**
conjunctivitis	결막염	**khyol mag yom**
constipation	변비	**pyonbi**
consumption	소비	**sobi**
contact	닿음	**thaum**
lense	렌즈	**lense**
contagious	전염병	**chon yom pyong**
cough	기침	**khichim**
cramp	경련	**khyong-ryon**
cure	치유하다	**chiyuhada**
cystitis	방광염	**pang gwang yom**
depressed	우울증	**oo-ul-chung**
dermatologist	피부과전문의	**phi-bu-gwa chon-mune**
diabetes	당노병	**thang no pyong**
diagnosis	진단	**chintan**

diarrhea	설사	**solsa**
disease	질병	**chilpyong**
dispensary	조제실	**cho sesil**
doctor	의사	**euisa**
dose	복용량	**phok-yong-ryang**
drugstore	약국	**yakh kuk**
dumbness	벙어리	**phongo ri**
dwarf	난쟁이	**nan zengi**
dysentery	이질	**yizil**
eczema	습진	**sub zin**
ENT	이비인후과	**yi bi in hu gwa**
Epidemic	유행병	**yu hang phyong**
Epilepsy	간질	**khanzil**
Faint	실신하다	**sil-sin hada**
Fever	열	**yol**
Filling	충전재	**chung-chon-che**

First aid	응급처치	**ungup cho chi**
Flu	독감	**thok gam**
Food-poisoning	식중독	**sikh zung dokh**
Gall-bladder	담낭	**tham nang**
Giddiness	현기증	**hyon gi zung**
Gland	눌림쇠	**nul limsuwe**
Glasses	안경	**angyong**
Gonorrhea	임질	**imchil**
Gynecologist	부인과의사	**puin gwa wesa**
Have cold	감기에걸리다	**kham-gi-a-kholida**
Headache	두통	**tuthong**
Heart	심장	**simzang**
Heart-attack	심근경색	**sim gun kyongzeng**
Hernia	탈장	**thal-jang**
Hiccup	딸꾹질	**tal-guk-chil**
High blood-pressure	고혈압	**kho hyol aab**

HIV negative	**에이즈음성**	**aezi umsong**
HIV positive	**에이즈양성**	**aezi yangsong**
Homeopathy	**동종요법**	**thong zong yo pob**
Hospital	**병원**	**pyongwun**
Hunger	**기아**	**khia**
Indigestion	**소화불량**	**sohwa pul layang**
Infection	**감염**	**khamyom**
Inflammation	**염증**	**yom zung**
Inhaler	**흡입기**	**hub ib gi**
Injection	**주사**	**chusa**
Injury	**부상**	**pusang**
Insomnia	**불면증**	**pul myon zung**
Jaundice	**황달**	**hwang dal**
Kidney stone	**신장결석**	**sin zang khyolsog**
Leprosy	**나병**	**nabyong**
Leukemia	**백혈병**	**paekh hyol pyong**

Madness	광기	**kwangi**
Measles	홍역	**hong-yok**
Medicine	약	**yag**
Menstruation	월경	**wulgyong**
Migraine	편두통	**fyon thuthong**
Mumps	볼거리	**pol gori**
Nausea	메쓰거움	**mes-kho-um**
Nosebleed	코피	**khofi**
Operate	수술을받다	**susurul patta**
Pain	고통	**khotong**
Pediatrician	소아과의사	**soaa gwa wesa**
Paralysis	마비	**mabi**
Penicillin	페니실린	**penicillin**
Pharmacy	약국	**yakh kuk**
Piles	치핵	**chi hekh**
Plaster	분말석고	**bun-mal-sok-ko**

Pneumonia	폐렴	**feryom**
Pregnant	임신	**imsin**
Prescription	처방전	**cho-bang-chon**
Pull muscle	근육이걸리다	**khun yogi kholida**
Pulse	맥박	**mekh pag**
Pus	고름	**khorum**
Rheumatism	류머티즘	**rheumatism**
Roundworm	회충	**hwichung**
Saliva	침	**chim**
Sanitary-napkin	생리대	**seng ni de**
Shiver	으슬으슬춥다	**usul-usul-chup-ta**
Shivery	오슬오슬	**osul osul**
Shock	충격	**chung gyokh**
Short sight	근시	**khunsi**
Sick	아픔	**aafum**
Side effect	부작용	**puzakh yong**

Sinusitis	부비강염	**pubi khang yom**
Sleeping pill	수면제	**sum yon ze**
Sneeze	재채기	**jechegi**
Sore throat	인후염	**in hu yom**
Sprain	삐다	**pida**
Sting	쏘다	**so-da**
Stomachache	위통	**withong**
Stool	의자	**euiza**
Surgery	수술	**su sul**
Sweat	땀	**tam**
Swelling	부기	**butgi**
Syringe	주사기	**chusagi**
Tablet	알약	**aal-yak**
Tetanus	파상풍	**fasanfung**
Thermometer	온도계	**on di gey**
Treatment	치료	**chiryo**
Tumor	종양	**chong yang**

Typhus	**발진티푸스**	**palzinthi fusu**
Urine	**소변**	**so byon**
Vaccination	**백신**	**vaccin**
Visiting hours	**면회시간**	**myon hwe sigan**
Vomiting	**구토**	**khuto**
Ward	**병동**	**phyong-dong**
Weak	**약한**	**yak-han**
Wheelchair	**휠체어**	**wheelchair**
Wound	**상처**	**sang cho**
X-ray	**엑스레이**	**x-ray**

Where is the pharmacy?
약국이 어디에 있어요?
Yak-guk-eaudiye yis-soyo?

Is there a night chemist nearby?
이 근처에 밤 늦게 까지 여는 약국이 있어요?
Yi khun-cho-ae pham nut-ke-kaji ya-nan yak-guk-gi esayo?

Is there a chemist nearby?
이 근처에 약국이 있어요?
Yi khun-cho-ae yak-guk-giesayo?

Where is the nearest hospital?
여기서 가장 가까운 병원이 어디있어요?
Yogi-so khazang khakaun pyongwani odi yissoyo?

Where is the casuality?
응급 처치실이 어디있어요?
Ung gup cho chi siri odi yissoyo?

What are the visiting hours?
면회 시간이 어떻게되요?
Myon-hwe sigani ato-khe thoye-yo?

Where is ward no 6?
6번 출구가 어디있어요?
Yuk- bon chul-gu-gaaudi esayo?

I need the medicine, please.
약 좀 주세요.
Yag chom chuseyo.

Please give me medicine to cure..
낫게 하는 약좀 주세요.
Nat-ke ha-nan yak chom chuseyo.

Is it available only on prescription?
이 처방 전에 만유효 한가요?
Yi cho-pang jan-e-man u-hyo-han-gayo?

I have the prescription.
저는 처방 전이 있어요.
Chonun cho bang zoni yissoyo?

How many times a day?
하루에 몇번 먹어야되요?
Haruwe myot bon mogoya dweyo?

Twice a day.
하루에 두 번이요.
Haru-ye thu boni-yo.

Have you taken this before?
전에도 먹어 본적이 있나요?
Chone do mogo bon zogi yi-nayo?

It is made according to prescription.
처방 전에 따라만들 었어요.
cho bang zone tara man duro soyo.

Can you order this medicine for me?
이 약을 주문해 주실수 있어요?
Yi yagul na aege chumun hal su yissoyo?

When can i pick it up?
언제 찾으러 올수 있어요?
Onze cha zuro ol su yissoyo?

It will be ready to pick up in 15 minutes.

15분 내로 준비 될거예요.

Sip-o-bun nero chu-bi-thyol-ko-yeyo.

I feel sick.

속이 안 좋아요.

Sogi-an cho-hayo.

I suffer from boils.

종기 때문에 괴로워요.

Chongi te-mune gwe-ro-wayo

I feel ill.

몸이 안좋은 거같아요.

Chega momi an cho-un go katha-yo.

I suffer from rheumatism.

류머티즘 때문에 괴로워요.

Ryu-motism te-mune gwe-ro-wayo .

You can buy it over the counter.
당신은 계산 대위에서 살수 있어요.
Thang-si-nan khe-san-the we-yeso sal su esayo.

Please get the doctor.
의사에게 상담 하세요.
Wesa aege sangdam haseyo.

Quickly!help! medical care!
도와주세요! 치료 가필요해요!
Tho-wa chu-seyo ¡ chir-yo-ga firyo-heyo ¡

Can i see a female doctor?
여자 의사를 만날수 있나요?
Yoza wesa-rul man-nal su yi-nayo?

I can't help coughing.
저는 기침을 견딜수 없어요.
Chonun khichimul khondal su obsoyo.

Are you on medication?
약물 치료중 인가요?
Yak--mul chiryo chung-in gayo.

I am on regular medication for..
저는 자주 약물 치료를 받았어요.
Chonun chazu yagmul chiryo-rulphada-seyo.

It would be helpful if you could come and see the patient.
오셔서 환자를 본다면 도움이 될것 같습니다.
o-syo-so hwan-ja-rul fonda-myon tho-oomi thyol-got kath-sumnida.

Which doctor is treating you?
어느 의사가 진료해요?
Onu wesa ga chin-ryo-heyo?

I cannot tolerate the heat.
저는 더워서 견딜수 없어요.
Chonun tho-wo-so khyon-dil su op-seyo.

The doctor prescribed complete rest.

의사가 절대 안정을 취하라고 했어요.

We-saga chol-the an-jong chu-e-haragohessoyo.

I will prescribe you a preventive medicine.

저는 당신에게 예방 약을 처방 할거예요.

Chonun thang-shin-aege yebang-ya-gul chobang hal koyeyo.

He hurt his hand.

그는 손을 다쳤어요.

Khununsonul tha chyo ssoyo.

I have a toothache.

치통이 있어요.

Chitongi yissoyo.

Where does it hurt you?

어디가 아파요?

Odi-ga afayo?

My head aches.
머리가 아파요.
Moriga afayo.

I don't have an appetite.
식욕이 없어요.
Sikgyogi obsoyo.

My stomach aches.
위가 아파요.
Wiga afayo.

Does it hurt much?
많이 아파요?
Man-hi afayo?

How do you feel?
기분이 어때요?
Khibuni otteyo?

I am constipated.
변비에 걸렸어요.
Pyon biye kholo soyyo.

I am dehydrated.
탈수증세가 있어요.
Chonun khonzo sikhyo soyo.

I fell down the stairs.
저는 계단에서 아래로 굴러 떨어졌어요.
Chonun khedan aeso aare rul torozyosoyo.

That made me sick.
그건 나를 아프게만 들었어요.
Khu-gon na-rul a-fuge man-dura-sayo.

Do you take drugs?
약 먹고 있어요?
Yak mo-go yi-sayo?

I have been injured.

저는 다쳤어요.

Chonun tha-chyo-sayo.

I have a case history of..

오래 전에 걸린 병이예요.

Ore-jane khol-lin fyong-yi-ye-yo.

You need to be admitted to hospital.

당신은 입원 할필요가 있어요.

Thang-shi-nun ib-wan-hal firyoga yi-sayo.

He needs a blood transfusion.

그는 수혈이 필요해요.

Khu-nun su-hyori firyo-heyo.

What is your blood group?

당신의 혈액 형이 뭡니까?

Thang-shine hyol-aegi muam-nikka?

Can you donate blood?
당신은 헌혈 할수 있어요?
Thang-shi-nun hyon-hyon hal su yi-sayo?

Please use a new syringe.
새주사기를 사용하세요.
Se chusa-gi-rul sayong-haseyo.

I think I am pregnant.
저는 임신했다고 생각해요.
Cho-nun imshin-hetta-go seng-gak-heyo.

Are you using contraception?
당신은 피임을 하고있어요?
Thang-shi-nun fi-imul hago yi-sayo?

Around the town

마을주변 (ma-ul chu-byon)

Around the town	도시주변	**tho-si chu-byon**
Airport	공항	**khong-hang**
Amusement-park	유원지	**yu-wonzi**
Antique shop	골동품상점	**khol-dong-fum sang-jom**
A one day excursion	당일치기여행	**thang-il chigi yo-heng**
Area	지방	**chi-bang**
Bakery	빵집	**pang-chib**
Bar	술집	**sul-chib**
Barber shop	이발소	**yi-balso**
Bazaar	시장	**si-jang**

Beach	해변	**he-byon**
Beauty parlor	미용실	**miyong sil**
Bicycle	자전거	**cha-jon-go**
Boarding house	하숙집	**hasuk chib**
Boating trip	보트여행	**boat yo-heng**
Bookshop	서점	**so-jom**
Border	국경	**khuk-khyong**
Botanical garden	식물원	**sigmul-won**
Bridge	다리	**thari**
Building	건물	**kon-mul**
Bus	버스	**bus**
Butcher's	정육점	**chong yug zom**
Shop	매점	**me-jom**
Café	카페	**cafe**
Candy store	사탕기게	**sang-thang-khi-ge**
Capital city	수도	**sudo**

Carpenter	목수	mok-su
Cart	카트	cart
Casino	카지노	casino
Castle	성	song
Cathedral	대성당	the-song-dang
Cave	동굴	thong-gul
Chemist shop	약국	yak-guk
Chinatown	차이나타운	china-town
Church	교회	khyo-hwe
Club	클럽	club
Cinema	영화	yong-hwa
Circus	서커스	circus
City	도시	thosi
City center	도시중심	those-chung-sim
Coffee shop	커피숍	coffee shop
Concert	음악회	umak-he

Consulate	영사관	**yong-sa gwan**
Corner shop	구멍가게	**khu-mong kha-ge**
Cornet	코넷	**kho-net**
Country club	컨트리클럽	**country-club**
Country	나라	**nara**
Cottage	작은집	**cha-gun chib**
Country road	시골길	**si-gol-chib**
Countryside	시골지역	**si-gol chi-yok**
Court	법정	**fop-chong**
Crowd	군중	**khun-chung**
Dairy farm	낙농장	**nak-nok-jang**
Dead-end	막다른길	**mak-darun khil**
Department store	백화점	**fek-hwa-jom**
Discotheque	디스코텍	**discotheque**
District	지구	**chi-gu**
Drugstore	약국	**yak-guk**

Dry-cleaner	**세턱소**	**se-thak-so**
Electrician	**전기기사**	**chongi-khisa**
Embassy	**대사관**	**thesa-gwan**
Excursion	**여행**	**yo-heng**
Excursion-train	**여행열차**	**yo-heng-yol-cha**
Exhibition	**전시회**	**chon-si-hwe**
Factory	**공장**	**khong-jang**
Farm	**농장**	**nong-jang**
Farmhouse	**농가**	**nong-ga**
Fence	**울타리**	**ol-thari**
Field	**밭**	**fath**
Fire-department	**소방서**	**so-bang-so**
Fishing	**낚시**	**nak-si**
Fish market	**어시장**	**osi-jang**
Flower shop	**꽃집**	**kot-chib**
Flower-show	**화초**	**hwa-cho**

Fort	**요새**	**yose**
Fortress	**요새**	**yose**
Fountain	**분수**	**bun-so**
Fruit shop	**과일가게**	**khwa-il kha-ge**
Furniture	**가구**	**kha-gu**
Shop	**가게**	**kha-ge**
Gallery (art)	**갤러리**	**gel-lo-li**
Garden	**공원**	**khong-won**
Gate	**정문**	**chong-mun**
Golf-course	**골프코스**	**golf-cos**
Granary	**곡창**	**khok-jang**
Grave	**무덤**	**Mudom**
Greengrocer's-shop	**채소가게**	**che-so kha-ge**
Grocer's shop	**식료품가게**	**sik-ryo-fum kha-ge**
Guesthouse	**게스트하우스**	**guest house**
Gutter	**홈통**	**hu-m-thong**

Harbor	**항구**	**hangu**
Hardware shop	**철물점**	**chol-mul-jom**
Hat shop	**모자점**	**moja-jom**
High-rise building	**고층건물**	**kho-jung khon-mul**
Highway	**고속도로**	**kho-sok-thoro**
Hill	**산**	**san**
Hospital	**병원**	**fyong-won**
Hotel	**호텔**	**hotel**
House	**집**	**chib**
Hut	**오두막**	**o-du-mak**
Inn	**여인숙**	**yo-insuk**
Jewellery shop	**보석류가게**	**pho-sok-ryukha-ge**
Kindergarten	**유치원**	**yu-chi-won**
Lane	**도로**	**thoro**
Landscape	**풍경**	**fung-gyong**
Library	**도서관**	**tho-so-gwan**

Liquor store	**주류판매점**	**chu-ryu fan-me-jom**
Lost and found market	**중고시장**	**chung-go si-jang**
Maternity-home	**조산시설**	**cho-san si-sol**
Ministry	**각부처**	**kak-fu-cho**
Mosque	**모스크**	**mosque**
Motorcycle	**오토바이**	**o-to-bie**
Mountain	**산**	**san**
Mountaineering	**등산**	**thong-san**
Mountain range	**산맥**	**san-maik**
Museum	**박물관**	**phang-mul-gwan**
Music festival	**음악축제**	**umak-chuk-je**
National park	**국제공원**	**khug che kong-won**
Nightclub	**나이트클럽**	**nightclub**
Optician's-shop	**안경점**	**aan gyong zom**
Orphanage	**고아원**	**khoa won**
Park	**공원**	**khong-won**

Pavilion	임시구조물	**im-si khu-jo-mul**
Pawnshop	전당포	**chon thang fyo**
Place of amusement	오락장	**o-rakh zang**
Plants	식물	**sigmul**
Poultry shop	양계가게	**yang-ge kha-ge**
Real estate	부동산	**pu dong san**
River	강	**khang**
Road	도로	**thoro**
Rural-dispensary	조제실	**chuze sil**
School	학교	**hakyo**
Seafood restaurant	해산물식당	**he-san-mul sik-dang**
Shoe shop	신발가게	**sin-bal kha-ge**
Shop	가게	**khage**
Stadium	운동장	**undong zang**
Station	역	**yog**
Stationer's shop	문방구	**mun bang khu**

Street	거리	**khori**
Street lamp	가로등	**kharo dung**
Street market	노상시장	**no-sang si -jang**
Swimming poll	수영장	**suyong zang**
Tailor's shop	양복점	**yang bog zom**
Telephone booth	공중전화	**khong zung chonhwa**
Temple	사원	**sawun**
Three wheeler	삼륜차	**samnu cha dong cha**
Ticket	표	**fyo**
Tomb	무덤	**mudom**
Tower	탑	**thab**
Town	도시	**thosi**
Toy shop	완구점	**wan gu zom**
Traffic	교통	**khyo tong**
Traffic jam	교통체증	**khyo tong chezung**
Traffic lights	신호등	**sin ho dung**

Traffic sign	**교통표지**	**khyo thong fyo-si-fan**
Train	**기차**	**khicha**
Travel agency	**여행사**	**yoheng-sa**
Tree	**나무**	**namu**
Truck	**트럭**	**thu-rokh**
University	**대학**	**the-hak**
Valley	**계곡**	**khe-gok**
Village (small)	**소촌**	**so chon**
Village (large)	**대촌**	**the chon**
Wall	**벽**	**pyog**
Wall (city)	**성곽**	**song gwak**
Watchmaker's shop	**시계기술자점**	**sige khi-sul cha-jom**
Youth hostel	**유스호스텔**	**yusu hosu thel**

Do I need to book?
예약이 필요한가요?
Ye-yagi firyo-han-gayo?

I would like to confirm my ticket.
제표를 확인하고 싶어요.
Che fyo-rul hwa-gin hago sifoyo.

It's full.
만석이예요.
Man-sogi-yeyo

I would like to change my ticket.
표를 바꾸고 싶어요.
Fyo-rul pakugo sifoyo.

I would like to cancel my ticket.
표를 취소하고 싶어요.
Fyo-rul chue-so hago sifiyo.

Two tickets for the tomorrow, please.
내일 자티켓 2장이요.
Ne-il cha thi-ket e jang-yiyo

Are children allowed?
어린이 허용 되나요?
o-rini ho-yong thoye-nayo?

Two child's ticket please.
아이 표 두장 주세요.
Ayi-fyo thu zang chu-seyo.

Is transport included?
교통비가 포함 된건가요?
Kyo-thong-figa fo-ham-thoyen-gon-gayo?

Do I need to take food with me?
음식을 가지고 가야되나요?
Umshik-ul khazigo khaya thoye-nayo?

Is lunch included?
점심이 포함 된건가요?
Chom-simi fo-ham-thoyen-gon-gayo?

Everything included.
모든 것이 포함 됐어요.
Modun gosi fo-ham-thyos-seyo.

I would like a guide book in English.
영어 안내 서가 필요해요.
Yong-o-ane-soga firyoheyo.

Do you have information on cultural sights?
문화적 명소에 대한 정보가 있나요?
Mun-hwa-jok myong-so-ye dehan chongbo ga yi-nayo?

I want to see local sights.
저는 지역 명소를 보고 싶어요.
Chonun chiyog myongso-rul fogo sifoyo.

Can we hire a guide?
가이드를 고용 할수있나요?
Guide-rul kho-yong-hal su in-nayo?

Where do we meet?
우리 어디서 만나요?
Woori audiye man-nayo?

When do we meet?
언제 만날 거예요?
Onze manal ko-yeyo?

When do we start off?
언제 출발 해요?
Onze chul-bal heyo?

Will we be seeing the too?
우리도 볼수 있나요?
Uri do pol su yi-nayo?

How much?
얼마예요?
Olma-yeyo?

When we do get back?

언제 돌아오나요?

Onze thora-o-nayo?

Can you recommend somewhere cheap but nice?

싸고 좋은 곳을 추천해 주시겠어요?

Sago cho-un go-sul chu-chon-he chu-si-ges-seyo?

Can you recommend somewhere luxurious?

고급스러운 곳을 추천해 주시겠어요?

Kho-gup-suro-un go-sul chu-chon-he chu-si-ges-seyo?

How long does the trip take?

여행하는 시간이 얼마나 걸려요?

Yo-heng hanun sigani ol-mana khol-loyo?

When does..open?

언제열어요?

Onze yoroyo?

When does..close?
언제 닫아요?
Onze thadayo?

Will we have some free time?
우리에게 한가 한시간이 있나요?
Woori-yege hanga-han sigani yi-nayo?

Will we be able to do shopping?
쇼핑 할수 있나요?
Syo-fing hal-su in-nayo?

Can you recommend somewhere romantic?
로맨틱 한곳을 추천해 주시겠어요?
Ro-man-thik-han go-sul chu-chon-he chu-si-ges-seyo?

What is the address?
주소가 어떻게됩니까?
Chu-soga otto-khe thoyem-nayo?

How long will we stay in..?
언제 까지 머물수 있나요?
Onze kaji man-nal-su yi-nayo?

Is it long route?
이건 먼길 인가요?
Yogon mon khorin-gayo?

What's worth seeing in?
보는 것이 뭡니까?
Pho-nun gosi muam-nikka?

How much does the admission cost?
입학 비가 얼마예요?
Ip-hak-phiga olma yeyo?

The guide has paid.
가이드 가지 불했어요.
Guide-ga chi-bul-hes-seyo.

Is there an English speaking guide?
영어로 하는 안내가 있나요?
Yongo-ro ha-nun aanega yi-nayo?

I would like to see the..
저는....를보고싶어요.
Chonun ......rul fogo sifoyo.

Can we look at today?
오늘 볼수 있어요?
o-nal fol-su yi-seyo?

When does the tour start?
여행 언제 시작해요?
Yoheng onze si-jak-heyo?

The tour includes two days in Seoul.
여행은 서울에서 이틀을 포함해요.
Yo-heng-un seoul-yeso yi-du-rul fo-ham-heyo.

Can we take pictures?
사진 찍을수 있어요?
Sazin chigul su yi-soyo?

What is this building/monument?
그빌딩/기념 물이 뭡니까?
Khu philding/khi-nyom-muri muam-nikka?

Who made it?
누가 만들었어요?
Nuga manduro-soyo?

What time does it open/close?
언제 여는지/닫는지알려주세요?
On-je yo-nan chi/that-nan chi al-lyo chu-seyo?

What is the admission charge?
입장료가 얼마예요?
Ip-jang-ryo-ga olmayeyo?

Is there a discount for groups?
단체 할인이 있나요?
Than-je harini in-nayo?

Who is the artist?
예술가 가누구예요?
Yesulga-ga nugu-yeyo?

It is a painting of his early period.
이건 그의 초기 그림이에요.
Yigon khu-ye cho-khi khurim-yi-yeyo.

Which country does it belong to?
이건 어느 나라에 속해요?
Yigon anu nara-ye sog-heyo?

It dates from fifteen century.
이건 15세기에 속해요.
Yigon yol tha-sot segi ye sog-heyo.

Could you take a photograph of me here?
여기서 저좀 찍어 주실수 있을까요?
Yogi-so cho chom chigo-chu-sil-su yi-sul-kayo ?

Why is the museum closed?
박물관이 왜 닫았나요?
Phang-mul-gwani we tha-thas-nayo?

Is it a national heritage?
국가 유산이에요?
Khuk-ga yusan yiyeyo?

Where can I find?
어디에 서찾을 수있어요?
Odi yeso cha-zul su yis-soyo?

Where are the toilets?
화장실이 어디에 있어요?
Hwa-zang-siri odiye yi-soyo?

We are just touring around.
우리는 방금 여행하고 있어요.
Woori-nun phangum yoheng hago yi-soyo.

I am lost.
저는 길을 잃었어요.
Chonun khirul yiro-soyo.

I have lost my group.
저는 저희 단체를 잃어버렸어요.
Cho-nan cho-he than-che-rul yi-ro-boros-soyo.

Where is the nearest beach?
가장 가까운 해변이 어디있어요?
Khazang kha-ka-un he-byoni odi yi-soyo?

Is it safe to swim here?
여기에서 수영하는 것은 안전해요?
Yogi-yeso suyong hanun go-sun aanzon heyo?

Directions

방향 (phang-yang)

English	Korean	Pronunciation
Straight ahead	직진	chik-jin
There	그곳	ku-got
Turn(n)	돌다	thol-da
Turn left (v)	좌회전	chui huijeon
Turn right (v)	우회전	ou huijeon

To face in direction

정면으로요.

Jeong-myon-royo.

Face this way!

이 쪽이예요.

Yi-chog-Yiye-Yo

Turn the corner.

모퉁이를 도세요.

Mo-thungi-rul tho-seyo.

Turn at the traffic lights.

교통 신호에서 도세요.

Khyo-thong sinho-yeso tho-seyo.

CHAPTER-24

On the telephone

전화 (chon-hwa)

Hello

여보세요

Ya-bo-seyo

Is Mr. Kim there?

김 선생님 계신가요?

kim son-sengnim-khesin-gayo?

Can I speak to..?

.....씨랑 통화 할수 있나요?

.... Si-rangthong-hwa hal su yi-nayo?

Speaking!

저예요!

Cho-yeyo!

Yes, i am Sasha. Tell me.
예, 저는 사사입니다. 말씀하세요.
Ye, chonun Sasha imnida. Mal-sum-ha-seyo.

Who is calling, please?
누구신가요?
Nugu seyo?

Whom do you want to speak?
어느 분과 통화하고 싶으신가요?
Ono-bungwa-thongwa-hago-sifon-gayo

Where are you calling from?
어디 서거셨나요?
Audi-sogo-syos-nayo?

I am calling from Seoul.
서울에서 전화하고 있어요.
Seoul yeso chon-hwa hago yi-sayo.

You have the wrong number.
잘못 거셨어요.
Chal-mot kha-syo-sayo.

What is your phone number?
당신의 전화번호 가뭔가요?
Thang-sine chon-hwa bon-ho-ga muan-gayo?

Could you put me through to Mr. Sidorov.
시도로브 씨를 좀 연결 해주시겠어요.
Sidorov si-rulchom yon-gyol-he chusi-ges-sayo.

Whose call is it?
전화 거신분은 누구세요?
Chon-hwa kho-sin bu-nun nugu-seyo?

What number do you want?
어떤 번호가 필요하신가요?
Ottan bon-ho-ga firyo-hasin-gayo?

Can I take a message for him?
메시지 남기 시겠어요?
Message nam-gi-si-ges-sayo?

Please tell him I had called.
제가 전화 했다고 전해 주세요.
Chega chon-hwa hetta-go jon-he chuseyo.

Could you give me the number ..?
전화 번호를 알려 주시겠어요?
Chon-hwa-bonho-rul alyo-chu-si-ges-sayo?

What is the code for India?
인도의 국가 코드 번호는 무엇인가요?
Indo-ye guk-ga khod bonho-nan muat-in-gayo?

Would you like to leave a message for him?
메세지를 남기 시겠어요?
Khu rul we-he message-rul nam-gi-go sifo-sayo?

Can I dial direct to Delhi?
델리로 직접 전화할수 있나요?
Delhi-ro chig-zob chon-hwa hal su yi-nayo?

I want to make an international call.
저는 국제전화를 하고싶어요.
Cho-nun khuk-che chon-hwa-rul hago sifoyo.

Please hold the line.
끊지 말고 기다리세요.
Khun-chi malgo khida-ri-seyo.

Where is the nearest public phone?
여기에서 가장 가까운 공중전화가 어디에 있어요?
Yogi-yeso kha-jang ka-kka-un khong-jung chon-hwa-ga audiye yi-sayo?

How much does a one minute call cost?
1분에 전화 요금이 얼마예요?
Il bune chon-hwa yogu-mi olma-yeyo?

Customs

세관 (se-gwan)

Can I see the passport, please.
여권 좀 보여 주십시오.
Yo-gwan chom foyo chu-sip-siyo.

Do i have anything to declare?
제가 신고 해야 될물건이 있나요?
Che-ga sin-go-heya thoyel mul-goni yi-nayo?

I have articles of my personal use.
이것은 제가 쓸물건 입니다.
Yi-go-san che-ga sul mul-gon-imnida.

That isn't mine.
그것은 제 것이 아닙니다.
Khu-go-san che gosi anim-nida..

Please open!
열어 주십시요!
Yo-ro chu-sip-siyo!

This is a present.
이건 선물 입니다.
Yi-gon son mul imnida.

I have cigarettes.
저는 담배가 있어요.
Cho-nun tham-be-ga yi-sayo.

That's my suitcase.
그건 제 여행 가방 입니다.
Khu-gon che yo-heng kha-bang imnida.

Do i have to pay duty on..?
세금 내야되나요?
Segum neya thoye-nayo?

It's a bottle of perfume.
이건 향수병 입니다.
Yi-gon hyang-su-phyong imnida.

It belongs to me.
이건 제 것입니다.
Yi-gon che gosi-imnida.

At the resturant

식당에서 (sik-dang-yeso)

Is there a good Chinese restaurant here?
이 근처에 괜찮은 중국 식당이 있어요?
Yi khun-cho-ye khwen-chan chung-guk sik-dangi yi-sayo?

Which restaurant is the cheapest here?
이 근처에 저렴한 식당이 어디 있어요?
Yi khun-choye cho-ryom-han sikdangi audi yi-sayo?

Is there a vegetarian restaurant here?
이 근처에 채식주의 식당이 있어요?
Yi khun-choye che-sik-chu-ye sik-dangi yi-sayo?

I would like to reserve a table for three people.
세 사람 자리를 예약하고 싶어요.
Se saram chari-rul ye-yak-hago si-foyo.

Are you still serving food?
아직 식사 되나요?
a-jik sik-sa thoye-nayo?

Where would you like to sit?
어디에 앉고 싶어요?
Audiye aan-kho si-foyo?

Is it self- service?
이거 셀프 서비스 인가요?
Yi-go self so-vise yin-gayo?

Waiter! / Waitress!
웨이터 / 웨이터리스
Waiter / waitress

Have you ordered?
주문 하셨어요?
Chu-mun-ha-syo-sayo?

What is the menú?
메뉴가 뭡니까?
Menú ga mu-am-nikka?

Do you have a menu in English?
영어로 된 메뉴가 있나요?
Yong-o-ro thyon menu-ga yi-nayo?

Is there family discount?
가족 할인이 있나요?
Kha-jok hari-ni yi-nayo?

I would like to see a drink-list.
저는 음료 목록을 보고 있어요.
Cho-nun um-ryo mog-rog-ul fogo yi-sayo.

We only want drinks.
우리는 술만 마시려고요.
Woori-nan sul-man masi-ryo-goyo.

How long is the wait?
얼마나 기다려야 되나요?
Ol-mana khi-da-ryo-ya thoye-nayo?

Is this seat taken?
여기 자리 있어요?
Yogi chari yi-sayo?

Some water, please.
물 좀 주세요.
Mul chom chu se yo.

Yes, I would like to have..
예, 저는..하고싶어요.
Ye, chonun …hago sifoyo.

I am on a diet.
저는 다이어트 중이예요.
Chonun diet-chung-yi-ye-yo.

I don't eat any meat.
저는 고기 안 먹어요.
Chonun kho gi aan mogoyo.

Is it cooked with butter?
버터와 함께 요리한 건가요?
Botte-wa ham-ke yori-han gon-kayo?

Could you prepare a meal without eggs/ meat/ fish?
달걀/ 고기/ 생선이 없는 음식이 가능 한가요?
Tal gyal/ khogi/ sang-soni ob-nun um-shi-gikha-nung-han-hayo?

Does it take long to prepare?
이걸 준비하는 시간이 많이 걸리나요?
Yi-gol chun-bi ha-nan si gani manhi kholla-nayo?

Two coffee please.
커피 두잔 주세요.
Coffee thu zan chu seyo.

Have you tried these..
이거 먹어 본적 있나요?
Yi-go mo-go-bon jok yi-nayo.

I love this dish.
저는 이음식을 사랑해요
Cho-nun yi um-shi-gul sarang-heyo.

This is superb.
이건 훌륭해요.
Yi gon hul-yung-heyo.

My bill. Please.
계산서 좀 주세요.
Khesan-so chom-chu-seyo.

Will you have some more?
더 드시겠습니까?
Tho-thu-si-ges-sum-nikka?

Ice cream with a banana flavor.
바나나 맛 아이스크림
banana mat ice-cream.

Is service included in the bill?
계산서에 서비스료가 포함 인가요?
Khe-san-ye so-bice-ryo-ga fo-ham yin-gayo?

10% service is included.
10% 서비스료 포함 됩니다.
Sip-furo so-bice-ryo fo-ham thoyem-nida.

We love the local cuisine.
우리는 토속 음식을 좋아합니다.
Wuri-nun tho-sok um-sigul cho-ha ham-nida.

That was delicious!
그건 맛있어요.
Khu gon masis-sayo.

At the Bar

술집에서 (sul-chib-yeso)

A doublé whisky.
더블 위스키.
Doublé whisky

Cheers!
건배!
Khonbe!

Do you like soda with it?
소다와 드시는게 마음에드 세요?
Soda-wa thusi-nan ge ma-ume thu-seyo?

Do you serve meals here?
음식 되나요?
Um-sik thoye-nayo?

Excuse me!

저기요!

Cho giyo!

Here's to you.

여기 있습니다.

Yogi-isum-nida.

How much is that/

얼마예요?

Olma-yeyo?

Its my round.

이번 술은 내가 사는거야

e-bon su-run nega sa-nan-goya.

I will buy you a drink.

제가 술을 살게요.

Chega su-rul sal-keyo.

The wine is extra.
이 와인은 추가 되는 것입니다.
Yi wa-e-nan. Chuga-thoye-nan gosi-imnida.

Will you have a drink?
술 마시고 싶어요?
Sul masi-go si-foyo?

Whisky with a splash of water, please.
위스키에 물을 타서 주세요.
Whis-key-a mu-rul tha-so chu-seyo.

At the hotel

호텔 (hotel)

Do you have any accommodation available?
방 있나요?
Phangi in-nayo?

I would like to book a room, please.
방을 예약하고 싶은데요.
Phang-ul ye-yak-hago sofon-deyo.

I have a reservation.
예약 하겠습니다.
Ye-yak-ha-ges-sumnida.

Sorry we are full up for / till.
최송합니다. 지금 방이 없습니다.
Cho-sung-hamnida. Chi-gum phangi ob-sumnida.

The hotel is booked up.
호텔이 예약 됐습니다..
Hoteli ye-yak-thoyes-sayo.

Please book us in for Sunday.
일요일에 예약 해주세요..
ir-yo-ire ye-yak-he chu-seyo.

For two nights.
2박이요.
Yi-ba-giyo.

Single room or doublé room?
1인 실이요? 2인 실이요?
Il in-si-riyo? E- in-si-riyo?

A.c.or non a.c.?
에어컨있는 방이요? 없는 방이요?
Air-kon yi-nanphang-yiyo? Ob-nan phang-yiyo?

Yes, check in here.
예, 체크인 하세요.
Ye, check-in ha-seyo.

What is the check-out time?
체크 아웃 시간이 언제 인가요?
Check-out si-gani onze in-gayo?

How much extra to stay until 9 o'clock.
9시 까지 있으면 얼마를 더내야 하나요?
a-hop-si-kaji yi-su-myon olma-rul tho neya ha-nayo?

Can I see it?
봐도 될까요?
Foya-do thoyel-kayo?

Its fine, I 'll take it.
괜찮아요.가져 가겠습니다.
Khwen-cha-nayo. Kha-jyo-kha-ges-sumnida.

Can I pay by credit card/ traveler check?
신용카드/ 여행자 수표 되나요?
Sin-yong-khad/yo-heng-ja su-fyo thoye-nayo?

Which is the room assigned to me?
어떤 방으로 주시나요?
Atton phang-uro chu-si-nayo?

Is there a safe in this hotel?
이 호텔 안전하죠?
Yi Hotel an-chon-ha-jyo?

Sorry, but the service is poor in this hotel.
미안하지만, 이호텔 서비스가 좋지않네요.
mi-an-haji-man, yi hotel so-vice-ga cho-ji an-neyo

Is service included in the bill?
서비스가 계산서에 포함 되었나요?
So-vice-ga khe-san-soe foham-thoye-go-at-nayo?

Yes, 10% service is included.
네, 10% 서비스가 포함 되고 있습니다.
ne, sip fo-sent so-vice-ga fo-ham-thoye-go yi-sumnida.

Can I leave my bags here?
가방을 여기에 둬도 되나요?
Kha-bang-ul yo-giye thu-wa-do thoye-nayo?

Is there a swimming pool?
이 근처에 수영장이 있어요?
e-khun-cho-ye su-yong-jang-e yi-sayo?

Just a momento.
잠시만요.
Cham-si-manyo.

Come in!
들어오세요!.
Thu-ro-o-sayo!

Could you come back later, please.
이따가 다시와 도되나요?
Itta-ga thasi wado thoye-nayo?

Did you call, sir / madam?
전화 하셨나요?
Chon-hwa-ha-syos-sayo?

Please wake me at seven.
7시에 깨워 주세요.
il-gop-siye khe-we chu-seyo.

Is there any message for me?
저에게 남긴 메시지가 있나요?
Cho-yege nam-gin message-ga in-nayo?

There is a parcel / letter for you.
여기에소포/ 편지가 있어요.
Yo-giye sofo / fyon-zi ga yis-sayo.

From where did it come?
어디에서 왔어요?
Audi-yeso was-sayo?

It came with the post.
우편으로 왔어요.
Wu-fyon-ro was-sayo.

When did it come?
이건 언제 왔어요?
Yi-gon onze was-sayo?

It came this morning.
오늘 아침에 왔어요.
Onul a-chime was-sayo.

When is breakfast served?
아침 식사가 언제 인가요?
Achim sik-sa-ga onze yin-gayo?

Can I use laundry?

세탁기 사용해도 되나요?

Se-thaki sa-yong-hedothyoe-nayo?

Can you call a taxi for me?

택시를 불러 주시겠어요?

Taxi-rul phulo-chu-si-ges-sayo?

Can I use your telephone?

전화를 사용해도 되나요?

Chon-wa-rul sa-yong-he-do thoye-nayo?

I am leaving now.

지금 떠나요.

Chi-gum to-nayo.

Did you have a pleasant stay?

즐거운 시간 되셨나요?

Chul-go-un sigan thyo-syos-nayo?

CHAPTER-29

Complaints

불만 (ful-man)

The shower doesn't work.
샤워기가 고장 났어요.
Shya-wa-gi-ga kho-jang nas-sayo.

Light doesn't work.
불이 안들어와요.
Phuri an thuro-wayo.

We will check it too.
그것도 확인 하겠습니다.
Khu-got-do hwa-gin-ha-ges-sumnida.

The door of my room no.202 doesn't close properly.
202호의 문이 정확하게 닫히지 않습니다.
yi bek yi hoye muni chong-hwak-ha-ge tat-ji ana-yo.

The window doesn't open / close.
창문이 열리지 / 닫히지 않아요.
Chang-muni yoli-ji / tat-ji ana-yo.

The lift is stuck at the seventh floor.
엘리베이터가 7층에서 멈췄어요.
Ele-veter-ga chil-chung-yeso mom-chua-sayo.

The air-conditioning/ fan does not work.
에어컨/ 선풍기가 고장 났어요.
Aircon / son-fungi-ga kho-jang nas-sayo.

The toilet is not clean.
화장실이 깨끗하지 않아요.
Hwa-zang-shiri kekut-hazi ana-yo.

The bathroom is locked.
화장실이 잠겼어요.
Hwa-zang-siri cham-gyos-sayo.

The room is too dark.
방이 너무 어두워요.
Phangi nomu odu-wayo.

The room is too cold / small.
방이 너무 추워요/ 작아요.
Phangi nomu chu-wayo / cha-gayo.

CHAPTER-30

Asking the way

길을묻는 (khi-rul mu-nan)

Am I right for the airport?
저 공항 가는거 맞죠?
Cho khong-hang kha-nan go ma-jyo?

Are we on the right way?
맞는 길이죠?
Mat-nan khiri-jyo?

Can I give you a lift for the airport?
공항 까지 데려 줄까요?
Khong-hang-kaji the-ryo chul-kayo?

Can you direct me to the market?
시장 까지 어떻게 가는지 알려 주실수 있나요?
Si-zang-kazi otto-khe kha-nun-zi al-yo-chu-sil su in-nayo?

How can we go to the shortest way to the monument?
유적지 까지 최단거리로 어떻게 갈수 있나요?
Yu-jok-ji-kaji choe-than-kho-ri-ro otto-khe khal su in-nayo?

How far is it to the airport?
공항에서 얼마나 걸려요?
Khong-hang-yeso olma-na khol-loyo?

It's a long drive.
여기서 꽤멀어요.
Yogi-so khwe moro-yo.

Is this the right place?
여기 맞는 곳이예요?
Yogi mat-nan gosi-yeyo?

Is this the road for?
이 도로가 맞아요?
Yi thoro-ga maza-yo?

Is it far?

멀어요?

Moro-yo?

It is on the other side of the street.

이도로는 다른 쪽에있어요.

Yi toro-nun ta-run cho-ge yi-sayo?

It is in the direction of..

~의방향으로

~Ye Pang-yang-uro.

It is 10 kilometers to the palace.

궁에서 10 킬로 걸려요.

Khung-yeso sip kilo-mitho khol-loyo.

This isn't the way to

~의 방향이 아닙니다.

~we phang-hyang-e anim-nida.

This road leads back to the hotel.
이도로는 호텔 뒤에 있어요.
Yi thoro-nan hotel thuyi-ye yi-sayo.

This road meets up with the motorway.
이도로는 고속도로에서 합쳐져요
Yi doro-nan kho-sok-doro-yeso hap-jyo-jyo.

This street leads to..
이거리가 ~로가나요?
Yi khori-ga ~ro kha-nayo.

Take the first on the right.
오른쪽으로 첫번째 길로 가세요.
Orun-chog-ro chot-bon-che khil-ro kha-seyo.

We have a long way to go.
우리는 갈 길이 멀어요.
Wuri-nun khal khiri moro-yo.

Where do we go from here?
여기에서 어디로 갈까요?
Yogi-yeso odi-ro khal-kayo?

Which is the way to the station, please?
기치 역으로 가는 길이 어디예요?
Khi-chi-yoku-ro kha-nan khiri audi-yeyo?

Which way to the airport?
공항으로는 가는 방향이 어디예요?
Khong-hang-uro-nan kha-nan phang-hyang-e audi-yeyo?

You are a long way out.
여기에서 너무 멀어요.
Yogi-yeso nomu moro-yo.

CHAPTER-31

Taxi

택시 (taxi)

Is this taxi free?
이 택시가 공짜 인가요?
Yi texi-ga kkong-cha in-gayo?

Please put the meter on.
미터기로 가죠.
mitho-gi-ro kha-jyo.

How much is it to..
~까지 얼마예요?
~ kazi olma-yeyo.

Please take me to this address.
이 주소로 가주세요.
Yi chuso-rokha-chu-seyo.

How much is the final fare?
최종 요금이 얼마예요?
Chui-chong yo-gumi olma-yeyo?

Please slow down.
천천히 가주세요.
Chon-chon-hi kha-chu-seyo.

Please wait here.
여기서 기다려 주세요.
Yogi-so khi-da-ryochu-seyo.

CHAPTER-32

In the police station

경찰서에서 (khyong-chal-so-yeso)

I have lost my passport / purse.
저는 여권/ 지갑을 잃어버렸어요.
Cho-nun yo-gwan / chiga-bul yiro-bo-ryo-sayo.

I want to contact my embassy/ consulate.
대사관/영사관에 연락하고 싶어요.
Cho-nun thesa-gwan/yong-sa-gwa-ne yon-lak-hago sifoyo.

I need a lawyer who speaks English.
영어를 할줄아는 변호사가 필요해요.
Cho-nun yong-o-rul hal chul phyon-hosa-ga firyo-heyo.

I apologize.
죄송합니다.
Joe-song-hamnida.

In the bank

은행에서 (un-heng-yeso)

Where can i ..?
어디에서.....할수 있나요?
Audi-yeso ....hal su yi-nayo?

I would like to cash a cheque.
수표를 현금으로 바꾸고 싶어요.
su-fyo-rul hyon-gumro pakhu-go sifoyo.

I would like to change money.
돈을 환전하고 싶어요.
thon-ul hwan-zon-hago sifoyo.

What time does the bank open?
은행이 언제 까지 여나요?
Un-hengi onze-kazi yo-nayo?

Can I arrange a transfer?
송금 서비스를 이용할수 있나요?
Song-gum so-vice-rul yi-yong-hal su yi-nayo?

I have forgotten my pin no.
비밀 번호를 잊어버렸어요.
Phi-mil-bon-ho-rul ejo-bo-ryos-sayo.

What is the exchange rate?
환율이 어떻게 되나요?
Hwan-yuri otta-khe thyo-nayo?

Can I see your passport, please.
여권 좀 보여 주세요.
Yo-gwan chom pho-yo chu-seyo.

CHAPTER-34

At the border

국경에서 (khuk-khyong-yeso)

Your passport, please.
여권 좀 보여 주세요.
Yo-gwan chom pho-yo chu-seyo.

Your visa, please.
비자 좀 보여 주세요.
Biza chom pho-yo chu-seyo.

Are you travelling in a group/ with family.
패키지/ 가족이랑 여행 중인가요?
Phe-kiz/ kha-jogi-rang yo-heng chung-in-gayo?

Are you travelling on your own?
혼자 여행하고 계신가요?
Honza yo-heng-hago khesin-gayo?

What is the purpose of visit?
여행하는 목적이 뭡니까?
Yo-heng-ha-nun mok-zogi mu-am-nikka?

I am on business here.
업무 때문입니다.
Om-mu te-mun-imnida.

I am here on holiday.
휴가로 왔어요.
Hyu-ga-ro wa-sayo.

I am here for 2 weeks.
저는 2주간 머물 겁니다.
Cho-nun yi-chu-gan mo-mul kom-nida.

I am nothing to declare.
저는 신고 할것이 없어요.
Cho-nun sin-go-hal gosi op-sayo.

CHAPTER-35

Socializing

사교 (sa-gyo)

Are you free tomorrow?
내일 시간 있어요?
Ne-il si-gan yi-sayo?

What are you doing this evening?
저녁에 뭐 할거예요?
Cho-nyoge mua-hal ko-ye-yo?

What are you doing now?
지금 뭐하고 있어요?
Chi-gum mua hago yi-sayo?

Would you like to go for a meal.
저랑 식사 할래요?
Cho-rang sik-sa-hal-leyo?

Can you come to dinner?

저녁에 올수 있어요?

Cho-nyo-ge ol su yi-sayo?

I will pick you up.

내일 데리러 가겠습니다.

Ne-il theri-ro kha-ges-sum-nida.

Are you ready?

준비 다됐어요?

Chun-bi tha thwes-soyo?

Yes, I am ready.

네, 준비 다됐어요.

Ne , chun-bi tha thwe-soyo.

Let me treat you to a drink.

술 한잔살게

Sul han-zan sal-ke.

Would you like to go for a walk?
산책 하러나 갈래요?
San-chek-haro naga-leyo?

May I join you?
저도 해도될까요?
Cha-do he-do thwel-kayo?

Ok!
괜찮아요!
Khwen-cha-nayo!

I feel like going out somewhere.
어딘가 가고 싶어요.
Audin-ga kha-go si-fayo.

CHAPTER-36

At the book shop

서점에서(so-jom-yeso)

An English newspaper, please.
영어 신문 주세요..
Yong-o sin-mun chu-seyo.

I need a map of the area.
지역 지도가 필요합니다.
Chi-yok chi-do-ga firyo-ham-nida.

Today's paper, please.
오늘 자신문 주세요.
O-nul cha sin-mun chu-sip-siyo.

I am looking for a joke book in English.
저는 영어 유머책을 찾고 있어요.
Cho-nun yong-o yu-mo-chek-ul chat-ko yi-sayo.

Small talk

한담 (Han-dam)

Good morning, sir/madam!
안녕하세요
An-yong-ha-seyo, son-seng-nim!

How are you?
잘지내세요?
Chal chine-sim-nikka?

Very well.
잘지내요.
Chal chi-neyo.

What is your name?
성함이 어떻게 되십니까?
Song-hami otto-khe thoye-sim-nikka?

My name is...
제 이름은......입니다.
Che yirum-un ...... im-nida.

Where do you come from?
어디에서 오셨나요?
Audi-eso o-syos-nayo?

I am from India.
저는 인도에서 왔어요.
Cho-nun Indo-eso was-soyo.

Do you live there?
거기에 살고 있나요?
khogi-asalgo in-nayo?

Where are you going?
어디 가세요?
audiye kha-seyo?

What are you doing?
뭘 하고 있나요?
Mu-al hago in-nayo?

What business are you in?
당신의 직업은 무엇인가요?
Thang-sine chi-gob-un mu-o-in-gayo.?

Do you speak English?
영어 할줄 아세요?
Yong-o hal chul aa-seyo?

I do not understand Korean.
저는 한국말을 이해할수 없어요.
Cho-nun hang-gug-ma-rul yi-he-halsu op-sayo.

I speak a little Korean.
저는 조금 한국말을 할줄 알아요.
Cho-nun cho-kum hang-gug-ma-rul hal-chul a-rayo.

Are you married?
결혼 했어요?
Khyol-hon hes-sayo?

Yes, I am married.
네, 결혼 했어요.
Ne, khyol-hon hes-sayo.

No, I am not married.
아니요, 결혼 안했어요.
Aniyo, khyol-hon aan-hes-sayo.

When is your birthday?
생일이 언제예요?
Seng-iri on-ze-ye-yo?

What is your age?
몇 살 이에요?
Myot sal-yi-ye-yo?

I am 25 years old.
저는 25 살이에요.
Cho-nun sumul tha-sot sal-yi-ye-yo.

What do you do?
당신의 직업은 뭐예요?
Thang-shi-nun chi-gob-un muo-ye-yo?

I am writer.
저는 작가예요.
Cho-nun chaga-yeyo.

Have you come for the first time here?
여기에 처음 오셨습니까?
Yogiye choume osyot simnikka?

How long do you plan to stay?
언제 까지 있을 계획 인가요?
On-ze kazi e-sul khe-wek-yin-gayo?

Another week/ two weeks.
다음주 / 2주.
Tha-um chu / yi-chu.

It is very nice here.
여기는 아주 좋아요.
Yogi-nun azu choha-yo.

It's been great meeting you.
만나서 반가워요.
Man-naso phan-ga-wayo.

Keep in touch.
자주 연락해요.
Cha-zu yol-lak-heyo.

With great pleasure.
매우 기쁘게 생각합니다.
Me-yu khi-ph-ge seng-gak-hamnida.

Whatever you like
무엇이든, 당신이 원하는대로.
Mu-at-e-dun, thang-sini won-ha-nan tero.

Ok.
괜찮아요.
Khwen-cha-nayo.

I am ok, thanks.
괜찮아요, 고맙습니다
Khwen-cha-nayo, kho-map-sumnida.

It's nice of you to help.
도와 주셔서 고맙습니다.
Tho-wa chu-syo-so kham-sa-hamnida.

I don't like that.

그걸 좋아하지 않아요.

Khu-gol choha-hazi ana-yo.

No thanks.

아니요, 감사합니다..

Aani-yo kham-sa-hamnida.

Wait a moment.

잠시만요.

Chamsi-manyo.

It doesn't matter.

상관 없어요.

Sang-gwa op-sayo.

Tomorrow is my last day here.

내일이 마지막 날이에요.

Ne-e-ri mazi-mak nari-yeyo.

I am here with my family.
가족과 같이 있어요.
Kha-zog-wa kha-chi yi-sayo.

This is my friend.
제 친구예요.
che chingu yeyo.

She is my wife.
우리 집사람 이에요.
Wuri chib saram yi-ye-yo.

He is my husband.
제 남편 이에요.
Che nam-phyon yi-ye-yo.

CHAPTER-38

Greetings

인사 (in-sa)

All the best!
행운을 빌게요.
Heng-un-ul phil-geyo.

And the same to you!
당신도요!
Thang-sin do-yo!.

Best wishes!
행운을 빌어요!
Heng-un-ul phiro-yo!

Certainly!
물론요!
Mul-lo-nyo!

Certainly not!
안됩니다. 물론 (아니지)
An-tho-yem-nida. Mul-lon (a-niji)!

Congratulation!
축하해요!
Chuk-ha-heyo!

Excuse me!
실례합니다.
Sil-le ham-nida!

Fine!
괜찮아요!
Khwen-cha-nayo!

Christmas greetings
크리스마스 잘보내요.
Khuris-mas chal pho-neyo.

Good!
좋아요!
Cho-tha!

Good morning.
좋은 아침이에요
Cho-un achim-e-a-yo.

Good afternoon.
안녕하세요.
An-yong-ha-seyo.

Good evening.
안녕하세요.
An-yong-ha-seyo.

Good night.
안녕히 주무세요.
Anyong-hi chumu-seyo.

Good bye.
안녕히가세요.
Anyong-hi kha-seyo.

Happy new year!
새해 복 많이 받으세요!
Se-he phok man-hi phadu-seyo!

Have a good trip!
여행 잘 다녀오세요!
Yoheng chal than-yo-oseyo!

Hope you have had a lovely time!
즐거운 시간 보내기를 바래요.
Chulgo-un sigan pho-negi-rul phare-yo!

How are you?
잘지내세요.?
Chal chine-seyo?

I am fine
잘지내요.
Chal chine-yo

I am pleased to meet you.
만나서 반가워요.
Manna-so phan-ga-wayo.

I see!
알겠습니다./이해 했습니다.
Al-ges-sumnida./ Ehe-hesum-nida.